DECODING 2012

DECODING

2012

Doom, Destiny, or Just Another Day?

MELISSA ROSSI

Library of Congress Cataloging-in-Publication Data
Rossi, M. L. (Melissa L.), 1965–
Decoding 2012 : doom, destiny, or just another day? / Melissa Rossi.
    p. cm.
Includes bibliographical references.
ISBN 978-0-8118-7327-7 (pbk.)
1. Prophecies (Occultism)   2. Mayas—Prophecies.   3. Two thousand twelve, A.D.
4. Twenty-first century—Forecasts.   I. Title.
BF1791.R68 2010
001.9—dc22

Manufactured in China

Designed by Supriya Kalidas
Typeset in Archer, Senator, DIN
Illustrations by James Noel Smith

10 9 8 7 6 5 4 3 2 1

Chronicle Books LLC
680 Second Street
San Francisco, California 94107
www.chroniclebooks.com

To

STEVE MEREDITH WARNER,
whose philosophical ponderings,
coffee-making skills, and wicked wit
added immensely to the creation of this book

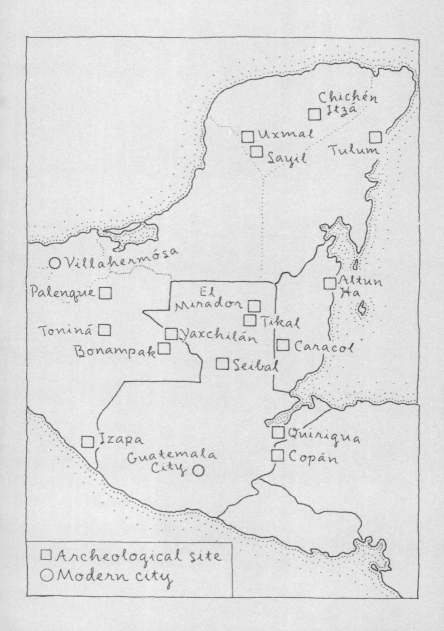

Chichén
Itzá

Uxmal
Sayil   Tulum

Villahermósa

Palenque   El
              Mirador   Altun
                              Ha
Toniná   Yaxchilán   Tikal
Bonampak   Caracol
              Seibal

Izapa   Quiriqua
    Guatemala   Copán
      City

☐ Archeological site
◯ Modern city

CONTENTS

INTRODUCTION

Bruce Scofield

The popular message of 2012 is that the Maya predicted catastrophic earth changes thousands of years ago. If you read this book, you'll learn that this "Mayan prophecy" is a much more convoluted affair. Many of the claims and predictions you might come across today have been drummed up by self-appointed, nonnative, pretend Maya "prophets." Most of these prophets draw attention to the number patterns in the several Mayan calendars that appear to be a code of some sort, and also the line-up of the winter solstice sun with the Milky Way. Some of them focus on 2012 as a time of doom and destruction, some predict a golden age and transformation of consciousness, and one even advocates that we change our civil calendar to one he invented that is based on Maya numbers. But the "news" about 2012 turns out to be a stream of very loose interpretations of an ancient astrological system, interpretations by people without any real understanding of astrology.

Astrology, a key element in understanding the Maya and the calendars that are at the heart of this debate, is an often misunderstood subject that bridges the gap between humans and the natural world. It is not a simple topic, and I will attempt to explain a few things about it as briefly as possible. In a practical sense, astrology is a mapping technique for dynamic systems. It correlates astronomical cycles with complex phenomena like climate, weather, culture, personality, and the human mind. Astrology, as I see it, hypothesizes that life internalizes astronomical rhythms, and it uses these rhythms as frameworks that structure activities. Astronomical cycles also map crucial transitions and tipping points in the lives of people, in cultures, and even in ecosystems. The usefulness of astrology is in its ability to link humans to the much larger natural world in which we live. It brings the sky to the earth, creating a vast framework on which time and change can be mapped and meaning can be interpolated.

Astrology originated in four distinct cultural areas—Mesopotamia, India, China, and Mesoamerica (ancient Mexico and Central America)—each with its own methodology, but all similar in principle. Maya astrology, a subset of Mesoamerican astrology, is largely based on cycles of the planets relative to the sun. A crucial component of Maya astrology is the 260-day tzolkin, a calendar that incorporates many astronomical cycles, including the appearances of Venus as a morning and an evening star, the cycle of eclipses, and the cycles of Mercury and Mars. In addition, Maya astrology considered the cycle of Jupiter and Saturn (about twenty years) to be a cultural and generational marker. This cycle was idealized to 7,200 days (called a katun), and it was used to map out longer periods of time.

The name "Mayan Calendar" is misleading. There were many Mayan calendars. When people talk about the "Mayan Calendar," they are generally referring to what scientific researchers call the Long Count. December 21, 2012, is the date that the Maya Long Count, a period of 5,125 years made up of 260 idealized cycles of Jupiter and Saturn, comes to a close. But, from an even larger perspective, the Long Count is one-fifth of an astronomical cycle called "precession," a wobble of the Earth on its axis that takes just under 26,000 years to complete. The Maya appear to have divided this cycle in fifths and charted the Long Count relative to the Milky Way, with 2012 being the anchor point of the entire cycle. This last fact is very interesting indeed. The next segment of this long cycle begins in 7137!

Does the Long Count shift in 2012 mark a shift in human consciousness or redefine consensus reality? Does Maya astrology actually work? On the micro scale, many have found the 260-day tzolkin with its twenty day-signs to be an astonishingly accurate gauge of human personality. The Maya focused on the cycle of Venus, especially its close conjunction with the sun, and correlations with flawed decision-making at these times have been noted. This current cycle of the Long Count is a block of time that began in 3114 B.C.E. and will end in 2012, with a midpoint in 550 B.C.E. We can't be too sure of what happened at the start of this cycle of the Long Count, although some scientists note rapid climate change about that time and history records a period of intense cultural creativity. At the midpoint of the cycle in 550 B.C.E., great men—Thales, Zoroaster, Buddha, Lao Tzu, and Confucius—propagated powerful ideas that continue to influence society today. Perhaps even now, as we approach 2012, we are in the midst of similar cultural developments, but it may take decades or even centuries before these might be able to be seen in perspective.

One way to interpret the end of this cycle of the Long Count is to consider it in the context of the Maya astrological system. By analogy with the 260-day calendar called the tzolkin, we are presently living in the last "day" of the Long Count, which began in 1993. This last "day" is symbolized by the sign Ahau, a sign that suggests a conflict between idealism and reality. It also suggests an effort to hold things together in the midst of contradictory forces—no small feat. The contrast between this "day" and the next one is striking. On 12.22.2012, the first "day" of the next Long Count cycle begins, symbolized by Imix, a sign of creation and the primal survival and nurturing instincts that keep life going. One could say that the boundary between these two signs is extremely sharp, a big jump from one state to another. This contrast doesn't suggest that the world as we know it will end—it suggests engagement in an accelerated process of change.

The book you hold in your hand is a guide to the madness of 2012 millenarianism—the human response to a perceived deadline in a time of uncertainty. Melissa Rossi's account of the phenomena leading up to and surrounding this date is a story of individual presumptions and social delusions, but it is also a sobering report on truly disturbing happenings. Her final words, based on solid data, point to the fact that we are indeed living in a time of profound transition. The take-home message here is that humanity has been the cause of its own problems. Waiting for "space brothers" to bail us out of our predicament, or for the glorious return of a golden age, is essentially collective denial.

The deeper problem in our current predicament is humanity's relationship with nature. We live in a world dominated by humans. Most of us are barely cognizant of the natural world around us—except as an annoyance. A large percentage of the human population live in desperate conditions, and these people have no choice but to regard the environment as something to be immediately exploited with no thought for the future. Many in the first world have become almost completely divorced from the natural environment in a different way. Electronic devices in homes, in offices, in cafes, and even attached to our heads, establish a fake alternate reality. The intense human subjectivity that arises from this situation makes dealing intelligently with the realities of our impact on the natural world very difficult. It is precisely this split of humanity from nature, long in the making but now pathological, that fuels the hysteria surrounding that deadline in time—the year 2012.

Astrology, the subject that links human life with natural cycles, is of value in such a situation. Mayan Calendar astrology might be seen as a cosmic alarm clock, jolting us into a greater awareness of our place in the biosphere and offering a wider perspective on our collective situation.

Whether or not you accept the idea that the Maya predicted that the world will change in 2012 is not important. The world is changing in front of our eyes. The arctic ice is melting, species are becoming extinct at the fastest rate since the demise of the dinosaurs, and human population growth is creating critical pressures on food supply and available land. These are troubled times indeed, and they call for more insight from our leaders than has ever before been required. Let's not sit by passively and wait for the arrival of 12.21.2012; we all need to embrace real change now.

01

THE TANGLED
WEB OF
2012

Spinning a Phenomenon

Dots chiseled on stones long forgotten in the steamy jungles of Guatemala and Mexico. Two-thousand-year-old letters describing ghastly visions. A black hole in the middle of the Milky Way. Global warming. A worrisome rise in natural disasters, pandemics, and killer diseases. Inscriptions on Sumerian cylinders and Egyptian pyramids. A sleeping supervolcano under Wyoming's Yellowstone Park that will challenge the planet's survival if it wakes up and blows. The revealing of 112 coded names to an eleventh-century saint. Pole reversals and holes in the magnetic field that shields the earth. Centuries-old drawings by Hopi shamans. Hallucinations of a medieval pharmacist staring into a chalice, predictions of a photographer uttered while in a hypnotic trance, and drug-induced visions of twenty-first-century scribes.

*Fig. 01_* COPAN IS THICK WITH SCULPTURES

An Internet word-tracking project. Ornate designs imprinted in fields. Hurtling asteroids, a "missing" tenth planet, and weakening gravity on this one. A panicked feeling of impending doom and the-sky-is-falling-itis. An unusual winter solstice when the sun supposedly lines up with the center of the Milky Way—an event that happens only once every 26,000 years. And, above all, the end date of an oracular 5,125-year Mayan calendar—heralded by New Age seers as foretelling a time of dramatic upheaval that could spell planetary doom.

Such seemingly unrelated phenomena now fall under the umbrella of "2012," a year being hysterically peddled as the time when civilization might go kaput and humanity could be violently erased from the Earth.

What not long ago was merely a year like any other is now a panic-filled global movement—a catch-all for every odd idea, unexplained occurrence, and kooky prediction, and a surprising selection of esoteric trivia from ages past. Whether the sources are astronomical, medieval, archeological, or Biblical or derived from Native Americans, Indians, or New Agers, the forecasts for 2012 typically follow one of two scenarios: instantaneous human evolution (apparently sparked as we pass through a highly charged beam) or cataclysmic ruin (apparently because of planetary positioning and because the Maya supposedly said it was so). Whether from giddy relief (*Yay, we will transform overnight into a more enlightened species!*) or deep dread (*Drat, humanity is entirely screwed!*), either message is capable of making a person stick his or her head in the sand, not a recommended course of action since, according to the 2012 message, there are only two years left.

The good news: Much of the information about 2012 that is flapping about is exaggerated, erroneous, or, at the very least, highly dubious—although that hasn't stopped many from being swept away by the 2012 wave of woe. The bad news: It's not so easy to shrug off some of the predictions, even if they originate from questionable sources. Scientists themselves are warning that, due to solar storms, 2012 could be one wild, shaky year, and problems—from climate change to increasingly likely nuclear showdowns—do challenge our survival. The other bad news is that the phenomenon of 2012—the idea that the world as we know it will be extinguished on December 21, 2012 (or 13.0.0.0.0, as the Maya would write it)—has turned into a dangerously powerful force; fear of planetary annihilation that year is working as a collective mood-shaper, despite the fact that the main actors who've planted that idea—whether drug-addled dream weavers, fame-seeking sensationalists, story-twisting televangelists, or scriptwriters whose "tales" are tailored for special effects—typically don't give a hoot about facts.

The ancient Maya have been elevated as the big stars of this show, but, as you'll see, even though their "prophecies" and their calendar are spotlighted as the sources for dire prognostications, this fatalistic movement actually has little to do with them. The casting of 2012 as a symbol for planet-wide calamity is the result of multimedia manipulation that has triggered a mass projection of fear in an uncertain time. The subtext beneath all the hoopla, however, is worth uncovering. As with any conspiracy theory—and 2012 in many ways is a conspiracy theory—there is at least a grain of truth to it, and this one might wreak a mess of havoc after all. Just not necessarily on December 21, 2012—and perhaps not even during that year, which promises to be memorable whether we get slammed by a comet, fried in a solar flame, swept away by a global tidal wave, or simply burned out from a heated election.

2012: SCHEDULED EVENTS

Whatever your belief system and whatever you know or don't know about the 2012 craze, one thing is for sure: The thirteenth year of the twenty-first century definitely won't be a snore—and not simply because Britain's Queen Elizabeth is planning to hold her fancy-schmancy Diamond Jubilee that summer. During this special year, humanity's first outer space hotel (the "Galactic Suite," complete with zero-gravity spa) is scheduled to beam open its doors. The world population is predicted to hit the 7 billion person mark and the price of oil (which is expected to hit its production peak that year) may surge well over 200 dollars a barrel, with consumers paying nearly 8 dollars a gallon at the pump. Nanotechnology—which manipulates subatomic particles and is already being used in everything from cosmetics to food to experimental weapons—is by then expected to be a booming multitrillion-dollar-a-year industry dominated by China, Japan, Russia, and the United States.

That year the Summer Olympics will kick off in London, and several ultrafast, next-generation supercomputers will be switched on, including one at NASA and another at the Department of Energy (to monitor nuclear plants and keep an eye on nuclear weapons). And 2012, which some evangelicals say will be the year when a religious government takes over in the United States,[1] also holds what is sure to be a heated U.S. presidential election, one which may see the return of Sarah Palin to the political ring (some predict that she will run on a presidential ticket with Dick Cheney).

The many international events already stamped on the 2012 calendar—from presidential runoffs to widely watched marathons—aren't the reasons why hundreds of thousands of people around the world are wringing their hands, building deluxe subterranean shelters, heading to sacred mountains, and moving into back-to-nature communes, or why psychics, gurus, doomsayers—and sellers of survivalist kits, weapons, and bunkers—are having a heyday. Thanks to Hollywood's hype, the History Channel's alarm bells, bogus assertions on the Internet, and a certain art history professor who claims to be a galactic agent/channeling telepathic/reincarnated Maya prophet-king—not to mention a flurry of puzzling articles and books—*2012* has become a buzz-word for "the End Times," "Armageddon," "the Apocalypse," and the termination of civilization by fire, flood, earthquake, volcano, nuclear war, solar flares, pummeling by asteroids, collision with a rogue planet, and/or alien invasion. It's the most sizzling nightmare topic to snatch headlines since Y2K, although 2012, should one believe the claims behind the ruckus, holds implications that make our previous worries about computer screwups look like tiddlywinks in comparison.

Most everybody who's chiming in as an expert about 2012 agrees that we're facing major shake-ups, societal changes, and planetwide transformations. The exact nature of what will unfold is the question. Whether 2012 will be filled with humanity-smothering planetary disaster, or mark a leap in human consciousness, or hold just run-of-the-mill global ups and downs depends on who you're listening to and what sources they're drawing from.

THE 2012 SHORT LIST

With everybody from UFO watchers to gurus weaving their interpretations into the 2012 fabric, and quotes (and misquotes) from historical figures (even the Delphic oracles and legendary wizard Merlin) embroidering the ever-growing crazy quilt, it's hard to untangle the individual threads of ideas. Here is the short list of commonly cited sources and concepts trotted out as "proof" that in 2012 human civilization is bound to unravel.

THE MAYAN CALENDAR The Long Count calendar kept by Maya astronomers—just one of their elaborate methods of keeping time—closes (actually it rolls over like an odometer) on December 21, 2012, marking the end of one cycle (called a "sun") of nearly 5,126 years. What the Maya felt about this event isn't clear: the sole "prophecy" that the ancient Maya left regarding the matter was written on stone that has since eroded and is impossible to read. (*See chapter 2.*)

JOSÉ ARGÜELLES, PHD The kingpin of the 2012 movement, self-proclaimed Maya know-it-all José Argüelles, wears many hats: He's a seventy-one-year-old psychedelic artist, former art history professor, author of bizarre books about space travels, and supposed channeler of a prophecy-issuing Mesoamerican monarch who died fourteen centuries back. Scorned by respected scholars, Argüelles nevertheless pulls a strong following among New Agers. Citing vague Mayan "prophecies" that warned about upcoming destruction, Argüelles laid the foundation for 2012 in 1987, when he put together the Harmonic Convergence; this gathering at sacred sites—to heal the vibrationally discordant world—was the catalyzing event in the creation of the New Age movement (see page 103). He has since devised a far-out lunar-based calendar and insists that we can save Earth only by changing our time-keeping methods and becoming more in sync with the galactic clock. Claiming a deep connection with the Maya (which most Maya deny), he predicts that "in 2012, the Earth will be in a condition of rapid, unprecedented evolution and change due to the enlightenment of the human species," which will come about after we adopt his Thirteen Moon/Dreamspell calendar.[2] The winter solstice of 2012 will launch an era of "oneness of humanity," "universal telepathy," and one world religion; with guidance from altruistic aliens, we will no longer need government, and the psychically charged crystals they give us will power nonpolluting "spiritual, telepathic fourth-dimensional technologies."[3] That's just the beginning: In 2013—a year that in his calendar is called "Yellow Galactic Seed"—we will experience the "great moment of galactic synchronization, the completion of the telepathic construction of Timeship Earth 2013 and the advent of the Planetary Manitou, the galactic brain on Earth"[4] —events that he hails as most welcome. He makes serious Mesoamerican academics howl: They say that his visions and prophecies have nothing to do with the ancient Maya; contemporary Maya elders agree. (See chapter 3.)

DANIEL PINCHBECK Hey man, trip out on what's about to unfold from the universal origami: we will soon alter our cosmic consciousness and ditch our "fundamentally flawed" concepts about the Milky Way—and how to behave in it. The energizing galactic era that kicks off when the Mayan calendar ends is sure to be groovy, says the author of *2012: The Return of Quetzalcoatl.* His book, offered "as a gift backward through space-time," draws insights from German philosophy, the Bible, insects, the I Ching, and strong hallucinogens to support his contention that we are barreling toward a major evolutionary leap. Scholars shrug him off as a navel-gazer, albeit a colorful one.

THE INSTITUTE FOR HUMAN CONTINUITY (IHC) This fake think tank, created as a marketing tool for the Sony Pictures movie *2012,* has scared the bejeezus out of millions with its pseudo-reports predicting that our planet is toast, soon to be torched by solar storms, and violently rearranged by crustal realignment, megatsunamis, chart-topping earthquakes, and/or a collision with high-velocity Planet X during that fateful year. Maya scholars, authors, scientists, high school counselors, and NASA scientists alike are alarmed by the appearance of the fictitious organization's fallacious Web site. Scientist David Morrison, who writes NASA's *Ask an Astrobiologist* column is but one lambasting Sony: he's been slammed by an avalanche of anxious e-mails about the IHC—including many queries from twitchy teenagers ready to kill themselves at the fake news of what's (probably not) in store.

PLANETARY POSITIONING, SOLAR FLARES, AND MAGNETIC MAYHEM According to writer John Major Jenkins, another star behind the idea of upcoming planetwide change, during the winter solstice of 2012 the sun will align with the galactic equator—the "line" that defines the exact center of the Milky Way; Jenkins writes that "this Galactic Alignment occurs only once every 26,000 years, and was what the ancient Maya were pointing to with the 2012 end-date of their Long Count calendar."[5] He believes that the lineup signals a moment when human civilization will be reborn, with the potential to take a giant step forward.

Alarmists have taken the idea further: They scream that this celestial positioning combined with intense solar activity will cause gravity to flip out and the magnetic poles to reverse, inflicting planetary mayhem. Some fear that galactic gravitational forces will provoke the huge, long-dormant volcano under Yellowstone Park, a caldera that lies under a third of Wyoming, to dramatically blow its stack, which it hasn't done for hundreds of thousands of years; others fret that Earth will be crispy fried in a mighty solar whoosh.

THE WEB BOT PROJECT Using software that was originally devised to forecast stock market trends by scanning the Internet for use of key words, the Web Bot Project is credited by its supporters with predicting the September 11 attacks and the blackouts of 2003. The project's founders recently predicted that 2012 would be an earthshaking year due to nuclear war and/or a reversal of the poles.

THE BIBLE Even though the Bible never speaks of the year specifically, the holy book keeps getting sucked into the 2012 debate, even though some evangelicals regard the Maya and the doomsday cult that's risen from their calendar as "Satanic."[6] Michael Drosnin, author of *The Bible Code*, which seeks clues in the Torah, says that for the Jewish Year 5772 (which stretches from September 2011 to September 2012), the Old Testament reveals the words "comet" and "Earth annihilated." Some preachers, including popular televangelist Jack Van Impe (and others whose videos can be found on YouTube), preach that 2012 is the year when the most horrifying scenes of the Bible may be acted out on the world stage.[7] They often point to the last book of the New Testament, the book of Revelation, which describes John the Apostle's vivid apocalyptic visions, regarded by many evangelical Christians as a play-by-play of "the End Times," which they say we're currently in. Revelation warns of coming plagues, the Anti-Christ, the Four Horsemen, and an era when nothing will be sold without a certain mark (which some believe is the bar code), in the lead-up to the return of Jesus Christ and the battle between good and evil. The book also contains a passage (chapter 20, verse 12) called the Final Judgment. *"And I saw the dead, great and small, standing before the throne, and books were opened. Also another book was opened, which is the book of life. And the dead were judged by what was written in the books, by what they had done."*

Some who believe that that these are the End Times also weave in Isaiah 24, which foretells God turning the world upside down (which some believe means a magnetic pole shift), and point to Luke 21, which warns of "men fainting from fear" as alluding to 2012. Jerry Jenkins, coauthor with Tim LaHaye of the equally terrifying (and best-selling) Left Behind books—which fictionally hammer home the ideas of the current era being the End Times—distances his works from the Mayan calendar but maintains that the clock is loudly ticking. "Everything we dramatized in the Left Behind books—the one-world govern-ment, one-world currency, threats against Israel—here it is on our doorstep," he told *Christianity Today*.[8] Christian author Mark Hitchcock, who wrote *2012, the Bible, and the End of the World*, is just one of those who link Biblical prophecies to the end of the Maya calendar—although he says he's just using the date, and his book, as a springboard to enlighten readers about the real-ity—in other words, Biblical prophecy.[9]

HINDUISM Seen by Hindus as the fourth cycle of humanity, the age of Kali Yuga—a period of discord, greed, and vice that began in 3102 B.C.E.—was traditionally held to stretch well into the future and last for 432,000 years. However, some swamis, gurus, and other Hindu spiritual leaders have recently revised the figure, saying that earlier figures miscalculated and that this unenlightened time actually ends in 2012. Those playing up the new date predict that the curtain drop will be tumultuous but will ultimately usher in a time of more divinely guided existence on the planet.

HOPI Paintings, legends, visions, and the Hopi Prophecy Rock— a centuries-old petroglyph in Arizona—predict that humankind is at a transition, hovering at the end of what Hopi (and other Amerindians) believe is the fourth world age, an era that will end in great devastation before a more enlightened fifth age begins.

One famous prophecy, the Nine Signs of White Feather, was revealed in 1958, when a pastor picked up a hitchhiker. White Feather, a Bear Clan elder of the Hopi tribe, told minister David Young of nine telltale events that foreshadowed "great destruction." The events were the coming of the white-skinned men, who "struck their enemies with thunder," the arrival of "spinning wheels filled with voices" (covered carriages), the crossing of the land with "snakes of iron" (railroads), "a giant spider's web" (electrical wires), and "rivers of stone" (roads), all of which had been fulfilled by 1958. The seventh and eighth signs—"the sea turning black, and many living things dying because of it" (oil spills), and the arrival of "youth, who wear their hair long like my people, [who] come and join the tribal nations, to learn their ways and wisdom"— are likewise considered "checked off." What's under debate is whether the ninth prophecy uttered in 1958—"You will hear of a dwelling-place in the heavens, above the Earth, that shall fall with a great crash, [and] appear as a blue star"—was fulfilled in March 2001, when Russian space station Mir fell from the sky.[10] The Hopi have never pinpointed 2012 as the year when human civilization goes up in smoke, but the fulfillment of the nine prophecies, said White Feather, would bring the end of the "fourth age" and usher in a period of disease, desertification, rising ocean levels, and horrible warring among those who possessed the wisdom of light (believed to refer to those in India and the Middle East) before a more harmonious fifth age could begin.

THE LAST POPE According to some sources, Saint Malachy, a twelfth-century archbishop, had a vision, complete with clues for identification, that Rome would fall and the Final Judgment would occur after 112 popes had come and gone—or rather 112 popes starting with Constantine II. We're currently on the 111th.

THE I CHING Used for thousands of years as a divination device, the ancient Chinese Book of Changes (a.k.a. I Ching), culls its lesson from nature and relies on the tossing of sticks or coins to produce six lines; depending on how the sticks or coins fall, the line is broken into two or a solid line, yielding a diagram with poetic prediction. Over all these millennia, nobody ever said the book predicted an end date. Until, that is, hallucinogen-gobbling Terence McKenna and his bro, Dennis, saw the book in a whole new light. Using fractals and drug-guided insights, they deduced that the Book of Changes revealed that all that could change in fact would change by December 21, 2012. Their controversial assertions have led some to announce that the I Ching also prophesied an end to the world—on the very day the Mayan Long Count calendar draws to a close.

EDGAR CAYCE (1887–1945) As an adult, this Kentucky-born photographer and game inventor developed a throat problem that rendered him unable to talk. Trying out hypnotism as a last-ditch effort to restore his voice, he discovered that, while he was in a trance, he displayed an ability to apparently tap hidden knowledge about healing, ancient civilizations, and the future. Cayce had a better batting average than most: He predicted the Great Depression, pinpointed the dates when both world wars would start and end, and foretold the deaths of several presidents—for starters. That's why his alarming forecasts of terrestrial changes—of the United States losing both east and west coasts due to earthquakes and tsunamis, and of a Japan that disappears under water, and of the melting of the arctic ice caps that causes rising ocean levels (the last a phenomenon now underway)—are given more credence than others. However, he never pointed to 2012 as the exact date when Earth's geography would be rearranged, and, in fact, the Association for Research and Education that he founded says he believed these changes would occur before 1998. (*See* "2012: Scenario Two—A New Dawn?" *page 33.*)

NOSTRADAMUS (1503–1566) Whether the medieval apothecary, who disguised his visions in symbolic poetry, was actually saying anything about 2012 or not, his name is often hauled out in the 2012 Hall of Fame. Believed by some to have foretold everything from volcanoes to wars, the rise of Hitler, and the breakthrough of penicillin, the seer definitely struck out in 1999: He had predicted that human civilization would go kaput that year. Like Cayce, he didn't specify the year 2012 in his prognostications; in fact his predictions stretch to the year 3797.

SANTA CLAUS Neither he nor Rudolph have uttered any predictions yet, but we're sure he'll soon join into the cacophonous 2012 chorus.

This certainly isn't the first time some have thundered that our world will be soon coming to a close. Whether the "end of the world" phenomenon is caused by societal stress—triggered by a shaky world economy, an exploding global population, diminishing resources, and strange weather—or stirred up by zealots and seers who foresee doom, prophecies by the hundreds have haunted human history.

A FEW WRONG CALLS

1/1/1000 Christian leaders across Europe predict death and pandemonium along with the return of Christ, launching wars against Vikings in preparations for Jesus' return. Widespread panic is averted only because few peasants can read, much less tell the time.

1843/1844 Preacher William Miller convinces his flock of 50,000 Millerites that Jesus will be coming in 1843 and that they no longer need worldly temptation. Many quit their jobs, refuse to plant, hand over heirlooms, money, and land to the church in anticipation and let their crops rot on the vines. At year's end, Miller confesses: He's confused the dates—Jesus will arrive on October 22, 1844. Even though he is a no-show then as well, Miller doesn't return the donated riches.

1891 In 1835, Joseph Smith, founder of the Mormon Church, predicts that Jesus will return in 1891, the same year sixteenth-century psychic Mother Shipton predicted the world would permanently flicker out.

1919 The alignment of six planets in December prompts warnings from respected meteorologist Albert Porta that the electromagnetic energy that results will cause the sun to explode and take our planet with it.

1953 The Egyptians, says author David Davidson, who studied the Great Pyramid for its secret messages, predicted the world would go bye-bye this year.

1982 The popular 1974 book *The Jupiter Effect* warns that too many planets on the same side of the sun will trigger massive flares and fry our electrical network.

1988 *The Late, Great Planet Earth* predicts a Rapturous year, followed by the end of the world, an idea mirrored by *Eighty-eight Reasons Why the Rapture Will Be in 1988*, which was penned by a NASA scientist. Both sell millions of copies.

The idea that December 21, 2012, will be a dramatic, possibly traumatic, date in human evolution has been floating around in New Age circles for a few decades. Several books in the 1960s and '70s mentioned the idea in passing, but several events of the early twenty-first century gave it new wings.

The horror of 9/11 followed by terrorist strikes in London and Mumbai, the mounting deaths in the wars in Afghanistan and Iraq, the Indian Ocean tsunami of 2004 that killed hundreds of thousands in minutes, the devastation in the wake of Hurricane Katrina the next year, the terrifying temblors in China, Pakistan, Chile, and Haiti that together killed hundreds of thousands more, the fluke tornado that ripped up Burma, along with pandemics, banking woes, dying bees, and the sudden tanking of the world economy, have all worked together to give us a feeling that the world is spinning out of control. And, in the past few years, we have been inundated with what some call "Y2-12," a panicky feeling that civilization is screwed, an idea that fits like a glove on the hand of 2012.

The date 12/21/2012 has now become synonymous with a fiery apocalypse. The year 2012 is the subject of more fanciful speculation than the dawn of the twenty-first century itself, gripping the world's imagination like nothing else before it, or so it seems. Dire predictions concerning what will happen during the winter solstice of that year have prompted some to begin burrowing underground, others to learn survivalist basics, and yet others to slip on T-shirts that glumly announce "2012: The End." But such fatalistic doomsday scenarios are only one take on the debate over 2012.

2012: SCENARIO ONE—DOOMSDAY AHEAD

Since the beginning of written history, and probably long before, some humans have been predicting the end of human history (see page 29), but never before have they had the use of so many vehicles—TV, the Internet, and mass publishing among them—to pound out the message. The year 2012 is being portrayed as one of cataclysms and nonstop disasters so horrifying they could blot out life from Earth:

- Solar flares will destroy our satellites, communication systems, and electrical network and fry our world in planetary fire.

- A catastrophic reversal of the poles will unleash devastating earthquakes and hurricanes, and tsunamis will topple cities and wipe them off the map.

- Supervolcanoes will destroy or drastically alter the atmosphere, perhaps triggering an era of darkness, a new glacial age, or an environment widely unsuitable for life.

- Nuclear war (some say between India and Pakistan, others say initiated by the United States, Iran, or Israel) will blot out life in most of the world.

- Rogue planet Nibiru and/or/a.k.a Planet X—which some say the Sumerians prophesied would "return" with disastrous results—will smash into Earth and utterly destroy it. Others say the cosmic projectile will just be a plain old comet.

- Some religious cults and psychics say 2012 (or thereabouts) will herald the arrival of extraterrestrials, who will guide us, say some, or take us away or overtake us, say others.

Whether they are survivalist doomsaying seers, Biblical prophecy camps, or simply movie directors hoping to churn out a blockbuster, many paint the year in the darkest shades of gloom, predicting extreme economic, social, and natural disasters. Pulling predictions from pretty much anybody who ever made one, some doomsters warn about changes so devastating that humanity, or at least those who haven't prepared, won't be able to survive. At least the evangelical Christian preachers who believe 2012 will be cataclysmic, such as televangelist Jack Van Impe, hold out hope for some, namely born-again Christians, who he says will be saved from the demise: they will be whisked up to the heavens during the Rapture.

While the most horrific interpretations of 2012 snag the biggest headlines, and fear has a way of catching hold more than hope does, there is another group studying the date who foresee the potential for an entirely different future. New Age visionaries are among those who see the year pointed to by Maya calendars as the time of a huge leap—when humanity reconnects with the Earth and develops a whole new packet of skills, among them telepathy and a doing away with our ability to lie. They say that finally humans will learn to live with each other and with the planet in peaceful ways. And their predictions are as extreme as those of the doomsayers.

2012: SCENARIO TWO—A NEW DAWN?

Contradicting the doom-'n'-gloomers, who paint a miserable, terrifying future, some New Agers and psychics, who might be dubbed "New Dawners," envision the year 2012 as the beginning of a new era of enlightenment.

While Edgar Cayce's "Earth change" visions are often cited by those who view 2012 as the end of the world, the heads of the institute that Cayce founded—the Association for Research and Education—say that, while he never pinpointed the year 2012, Cayce believed that around that time we would enter a new era of "purity," evolved "global consciousness," and heightened spirituality, which would allow us to more clearly communicate with the Creator(s), whomever one envisions that to be.

New Age luminaries such as José Argüelles see 2012 in terms of rainbows: In preparation for our upcoming evolutionary leap—guided by aliens—Argüelles is already gathering known psychics and sending them to sacred sites, where they are serving as "telepathic batteries." He says that by envisioning rainbows encircling the globe, they will produce a positive revolution with a beneficial result as mighty as nuclear war. He sees what is happening as a crucial step in the development of human spirituality, ending our path toward domination by machines, in order to create a future when humans live without war or lies. Daniel Pinchbeck, author of *2012: The Return of Quetzalcoatl*, considers crop circles and reports of alien abductions as a few indicators of a coming global shift and species transcendence. He predicts that, instead of the end of the world, we will see the opening of a new one that will reorder our incorrect notions of time, space, and spirit. John Major Jenkins, who helped popularize the Mayan calendar and its "end date," also sees it as a time of renewal, when humanity can tap lost wisdom and open a "door into the heart of space of time."[11]

Whether they are painted by Apocalyptics or New Dawners, many 2012 scenarios appear to have fallen out of a sci-fi novel or a religious thriller or be the result of eating way too many psychedelic mushrooms. But the oddest thing about the whole 2012 craze is that it can't be entirely laughed off as the tales of outlandish nuts. The "event" weaves together ancient prediction, astronomy, archeology, science, religion, meteorology, high-tech advances, and hard cold fact; trying to figure out where one stops and the other starts can be the difficult part of figuring out what 2012 really means. As "far-out" as assorted scenarios may sound, at least some of the concerns about 2012 and the issues it raises appear to be rooted in reality.

While the doomsayers and the New Dawners offer the most colorful forecasts of 2012, there is another interested group that doesn't look at the exact year or the Mayan calendar per se but says that we have entered an era when human civilization may indeed be coming to a crossroads. This group, made up of some scientists, futurists, astrophysicists, humanist philosophers, environmentalists, and demographers, offers some of the most intriguing information and sometimes alarming scenarios.

2012: SCENARIO THREE—CROSSROADS AHEAD?

Nobody, not even our finest scientists, can foretell exactly what lies in our future. However, some are issuing warnings and forecasts pointing out potential problems ahead.

▶ In 2008, the esteemed National Academy of Sciences (NAS) issued a lengthy report, "Severe Space Weather Events: Understanding Societal and Economic Impacts." In the NASA-funded report, the authors warn of the destructive capabilities of "episodes of severe space weather [such as] the geomagnetic superstorms of March 1989," when a solar superstorm knocked out the Quebec power grid leaving 6 million across Canada without power on a frigid day. They also reminded of the damage inflicted by ghoulish solar flares that fried satellites and photo-snapping spacecraft in autumn of 2003. The NAS report forecasts much more extreme storms in the near future and predicts catastrophic effects for our electrical system. Regional blackouts, even nationwide blackouts, and destruction of transformers could cost trillions of dollars and take years to repair. The report urges utilities to prepare for these upcoming events.[12]

▶ In December 2008, NASA reported that there is a gaping hole, four times bigger than Earth itself, in the magnetosphere that surrounds our planet and acts as a protective shield against harmful solar winds and the solar "plasma" that shoots out during solar storms. Nobody seems quite sure what consequences this could have, but it doesn't look good for 2012—a year NASA predicts will have a large number of solar flares.

➤ The U.S. Geological Survey of the Department of the Interior published a report in 2007 that assesses "future violent events" in Yellowstone National Park. Depending on what happens in this volcanic system, 70,000 people or more could be affected; if the supervolcano system running under the park violently erupted, it could dramatically affect the entire North American continent or beyond.[13]

➤ While some still debate the causes of climate change, most scientists believe it is a result of greenhouse gases emitted by cars, planes, factories, and our homes and workplaces—not to mention emissions from our rockets. In any case, we can measure that it is happening. One yardstick is the declining thickness and range of arctic ice caps and the accompanying rise in sea levels. Sea levels have already risen 2 inches since 1995, and by some estimates they will rise by over 7 feet by the end of the century.[14] Such changes will ultimately spell the end of low-lying areas such as the Maldives, a vast island chain in the Indian Ocean. The president of the Maldives is so alarmed that he recently held an underwater press conference to highlight the Maldivian archipelago of tomorrow, and he is shopping to buy land for a new country.

➤ In 2005, amid reports that a fast-moving asteroid called 2004 MN4 might hit Earth with catastrophic effect on April 13, 2029, NASA issued a statement that it would be a close call, but that it would miss.[15] Other scientists, including those who first spotted the asteroid, aren't quite so convinced.

➤ In 2002, NASA reported a mysterious change in the gravitational field on our planet,[16] and for years, reports have indicated a gradual drifting of the magnetic poles—the North Pole, for example, has been moving toward Siberia over the past century. What exactly this means is also up for debate, but some scientists speculate that indeed the poles may reverse—although probably not for centuries.

Even those who shrug off 2012 as mumbo jumbo—and there are plenty of skeptics—would probably admit that these appear to be unusual times. The tsunami of 2004 that killed over 230,000 people, a series of earthquakes that recently rocked Asia and Haiti, fluke hurricanes, and a series of strange weather events do appear to indicate something is up—although these events, or some of them, may be the results of weapons testing. (See chapter 3.) Whether looking at this era from the perspective of a New Ager, Christian, Jew, Hindu, psychic, humanist, scientist, or concerned inhabitant of Earth, it appears we may be at the threshold of something big. And most who are scrutinizing the near future, be it the December solstice of 2012 or a less specific date, believe that the survival of humanity now hinges on the choices made by those living on the planet right now.

Before looking at exactly who is shaping this 2012 "event" and examining the "scientific facts" surrounding it, we'll start with a look at the past and the curious case of the Maya—the Mesoamerican Indians whose calendar, say some, indicates that 2012 isn't going to be just any old year.

THE
MYSTICAL
MADDENING
MAYA
The Timekeepers' Mysteries

The mysterious Maya lie at the heart of the 2012 craze. That's no surprise. The long-ago civilization of warring magicians, star-gazing mathematicians, and hallucinating shaman-kings refuses to fade gracefully into the pages of history. Other cultures from the past—the alphabet-giving Phoenicians, for instance—appear content to crawl off and be forgotten. Not the ancient Maya, who keep rattling the windows of our world— a thousand years after their own vanished. Never before has a long-gone culture been more in our face, continually grabbing headlines, triggering social trends, and shaking up our lives with their lost knowledge. No other people of the past has proved so capable of driving modern men mad.

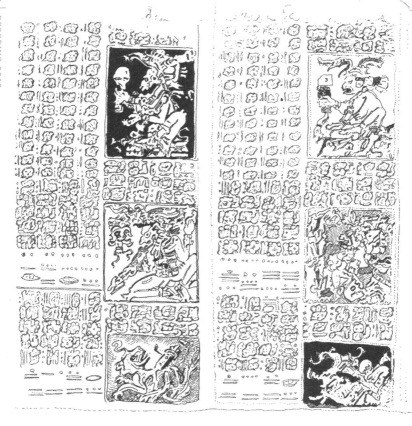

Fig.02_ DRESDEN CODEX

Written in the fourteenth century and smuggled to Europe by Spanish conquistador Hernán Cortés, this folded-bark book of Mayan hieroglyphics became known as the Dresden Codex, for the city in Germany where it surfaced in 1744. Penned by Maya shamans, the accordion-like seventy-eight pages are filled with star tables, histories of floods and kings, and myths—but no prophecies about 2012, say scholars. The Maya held thousands of books in their libraries, but the Dresden Codex is one of only four believed to have survived the bonfires of conversion-happy Spanish priests in 1562. The Dresden Codex divulged crucial clues to the Mayan number system, their studies of planets, and their most unusual calendars.

Then again, the Classic Maya, as those who lived in city-states across Central America between 300 and 900 C.E. were known, were a spirited, strange, and unusual bunch. They were fond of fortune-telling, tripped-out séances, public self-mutilation, and heart-ripping sacrifices during which blood was splattered about like holy water. Occult exploration was encouraged—shamans attended magicians' schools to learn star mapping, day counting, and spell casting—and numbers, believed to hold magical properties, were used to chart planets, map time, and plot geometrically perfect monuments. Maya kings were believed to channel the gods, who gave them advice on everything from war to weather, while shamans, who carried sacred pouches of seeds, shells, and magnets, were believed to be "shapeshifters," capable of transforming into jaguars, eagles, and snakes.

One thing is clear: The Classic Maya certainly knew how to disappear. After emptying their cities around 930 C.E., remnants of their culture vanished in the tropical rainforest. Even their descendants—the millions of Maya who still live in Guatemala and Mexico—knew little of their forbearers' dramatic civilization or where their emptied cities lay hidden. The discovery of other lost cultures, while fascinating, rarely rates more than a cover story in *Archeology Today*; the ancient Maya, however, keep popping up and altering our world—often quite dramatically. And that's how it's been ever since the 1800s, when explorers first stumbled into the Mayan hidden cities of towering pyramids, where they pried open sacred temples, unearthed tombs sealed with spells, and woke up the sleeping sorcerer-kings.

Discovery of their forgotten civilization shook up nineteenth-century society and unleashed fantastical theories of all sorts, starting with furious conjecturing about just who these strange people were. Over the past two hundred years, the Maya have been held up as descendants of everyone from the lost tribes of Israel to survivors of mythical lands to colonizers from other galaxies. Their masterfully designed monuments drew comparisons to the Freemasons, their intricate timekeeping devices offered more ways to measure the movement of days and planets than had ever been previously conceived. Startled Harvard professors hailed the Maya as revolutionary thinkers who were thirteen centuries ahead of Einstein in comprehending the meaning of time's relativity.

Museums and scholarly institutions sank billions of dollars into excavating Maya treasures, documenting their stylized art, and attempting to decode their language; books about their jungle-swallowed cities were instant best-sellers. Public lectures about these mysterious Mesoamericans were standing-room-only affairs that sent early-twentieth-century high society into a heart-fluttering tizzy; the Maya (and their supposed ancestors, the Atlanteans) were the talk of the town. Hero aviator Charles Lindbergh swooped over jagged volcanic mountains searching for lost Mayan ruins, his daring stunts making the front pages of newspapers worldwide.

Forget the Egyptians—who, while mesmerizing, were more or less understood—and never mind the Aztec, a much younger culture even more prone to warring. The Maya were different: Clearly advanced, but utterly mysterious, these sorcerer-astronomer-artist-magus-mathematicians taunted modern humans by leaving messages all over the place—in mural-wrapped tombs, up pyramid stairs, across stone monuments—but writing them in hieroglyphs that were all but impossible to understand. Those who did study their meaning sometimes went nuts, literally.

In all the hoopla they stirred up, the ancient Maya inadvertently spurred major innovations and triggered social movements, from the creation of the Panama Canal—the New World's most daring engineering feat—to playing an accidental role in launching World War II. (See pages 72 to 79.) Even now, despite continuing to be really quite dead, the Classic Maya can't stay out of the news, since sensationalists can't stop wheeling out this omen-obsessed and calendar-happy culture as proof of everything from extraterrestrial communication to the existence of Atlantis. Lately, the sleeping ancients have been roused yet again and shoved in front of the camera, this time as "proof" of 2012 theories.

The Classic Maya are the twenty-first century's most colorful voice of doom, the ominous source, it's widely believed, of dire predictions based on a time-telling device that marks the day when our world will end. Phrases such as "according to ancient Mayan prophecy" and "the end of the Mayan calendar" are now shorthand for "doomsday," and the messengers of gloom are suddenly omnipresent: the Classic Maya are movie stars, the subject of documentaries, books, articles, and ad campaigns.

The ancients' supposed predictions—and the ominous implication in the ending of their 5,125-year Long Count calendar on December 21, 2012, a date that marks the ending of thirteen baktuns—have been firmly stamped into the world's unconscious via the Internet, radio, books, TV, and big-money movie productions of the slickest variety. Sony Pictures' chilling, if plot-thin, *2012* showed a planet swept away in tsunamis and continent-cracking earthquakes—events portrayed as though foretold by the ancient Maya. "Mankind's earliest civilization warned us!" announced the movie's disturbing trailer, deftly weaving together two whoppers: Not only is it questionable to assert that the

*Fig.03*_LONG COUNT DATE 12.19.19.17.19

Those who believe that the date 13.0.0.0.0 on the Mayan Long Count calendar signifies the last dance of humanity might wish to celebrate the day before, as the "End of the World's Eve." The latter date, written as 12.19.19.17.19, symbolizes 12 baktun (each baktun measures about 144,000 days), 19 katun (each katun measures 7,200 days), 19 tun (each tun measures 360 days), 17 uinals (each uinal measures 20 days) and 19 kin—or days. Each of the symbols to the right of the number (dots and bars) signify a period of time (baktun, katun, etc.). The last two symbols on the bottom signify the "calendar round" date. Using base twenty instead of base ten, the long count stretches 1,872,000 days or 5,125.37 years. (See "Time Matters," page 80.)

Maya forewarned us about anything, the statement also betrays the moviemakers' alarming unfamiliarity with history—overlooking the many civilizations (in Egypt, Mesopotamia, China, and the Indus Valley for starters) that preceded the Maya. A few years earlier, Mel Gibson's violent and gory *Apocalypto*, about the collapse of the Classic Maya civilization, held an allegory of environmental limit bashing: Believing that weather changes, crop failures, and economic decline could be halted only by building more temples, Maya leaders of the tenth century entirely denuded the last forests—hammering in the final nail of their coffin, while foreshadowing ours.

The future-telling Maya are sizzling celebs on the History Channel, where sky-is-falling specials are so popular that the former "All-Vietnam Channel" has been repackaged into non-stop "The apocalypse is near TV." The Maya and their doom-foretelling device are snagging long features in magazines from *Playboy* to the *New York Times Magazine*; the ancients have been successfully branded as the leading experts on the looming apocalypse, despite the fact that they can no longer talk.

What's specifically causing the worry is the Long Count calendar, one of several Mayan day-counting devices. Originally developed by the Maya's neighbors, the star-gazing Olmec, this calendar that spans 5,125 years was used to track eclipses, lunar phases, Venus transits, and other heavenly activities thousands of years into the past and future. Ignored by the public for centuries, the Long Count calendar is now snagging headlines for one reason: It comes to a screeching halt on the winter solstice of December 21, 2012. And we're continually told that the calendar's turnover date, written as 13.0.0.0.0, marks the day that "according to the ancient Maya" is synonymous with the grand finale of our planet. (See "Time Matters," page 80.)

There's only one problem with the recent recasting of the Maya as spokesmen for the coming apocalypse: According to the foremost Maya scholars, the ancient Maya never gonged that gloomy death knell while they were alive. Despite what you can read everywhere on the Internet, despite what certain New Age seers inform us or what's stated in movies and implied in books, the Classic Maya left no writings that prophesy planetary demise in our time—nor did they say that the end of the Long Count calendar marks the tragic moment. To judge by the thousands of inscriptions they chiseled on stone columns (stela) and painted on monument walls, the ancient Maya didn't give much thought at all to the date when the Long Count calendar rolls over odometer-style to 13.0.0.0.0, signifying the end of the thirteenth baktun. To reiterate: The ancient Maya never once said the Long Count calendar's end date spelled the end of the world. (See chapter 3.)

Then again, they didn't say it wasn't the end either. The Maya, it's true, were known to vacate their cities on some "turnover" dates;[17] for other "turnover" dates they threw citywide bashes of drinking, dancing, fervent sacrificing, and elaborate monument building. What the ancients believed about the rollover date of the Long Count in 2012, or if they even dwelled on it at all, is a big question mark, according to Professor David Stuart of the University of Texas at Austin, a leading Maya expert and son of a famous archeologist, who's lived and breathed Maya since he was a toddler. (See "Code Crackers," page 95.)

Stuart says that we cannot read even one prophecy about 13.0.0.0.0 on any ancient Mayan temples, ball courts, tombs, palace paintings, or stone markers. "There is one monument erected by a minor king who ruled over a minor city that begins, 'when the 13th baktun ends . . . ' But the monument is cracked, and the rest of the glyphs are missing or undecipherable." Outside of that stela—so-called Monument 6 in Tortuguero in Mexico—the absolute lack of attention given the matter of the calendar end date signals to Stuart and other scholars that the rollover of the Long Count—a date that lay over a thousand years in their future—was neither an issue for the Maya nor a source of fascination. "The Maya cared about their time, not ours," says Stuart. "The Classic Maya were not leaving messages for us."

Perhaps not, but the ancients were certainly leaving messages everywhere—on tombs, temples, and stone markers. It's just that until the last thirty years we had no idea what they meant, since Mayan hieroglyphics proved surprisingly difficult to decode. Only since the late 1970s—with help from Stuart—have we had much of a clue what the Mayan hieroglyphic communications were saying. Turns out most were family trees and biographies in stone.

THE ANCIENT MAYA: WHO WERE THEY?

Peel back the feathered serpent masks, the occult schools, the planet-aligned architecture . . . and you find a kernel of corn. The Mayan culture grew out of it: Cultivation of maize, by far their most important crop, allowed populations to swell, cities to grow, and trade to flourish. Even the Mayan creation myth, the Popol Vuh, claims that the Maya were created from the starchy vegetable—previous experiments with mud and wood, it was believed, had produced inferior beings who didn't worship their creators and thus had been destroyed. Only when fashioned from maize, says the myth, were the Maya duly respectful, making sacrifices to the deities, particularly those who controlled agriculture, the gods of sun, rain, and corn.

*Fig.04_*SCULPTURES OF MAYA LEADERS
GREETED MYSTIFIED EXPLORERS

The foundation of Mayan society was laid on the crop. Along with mastery of irrigation, cultivation of corn across the mountainous terrain and lowlands of southern Mexico, Guatemala, Belize, and Honduras, as well as the Yucatán peninsula, created a food surplus that spurred urbanization and the rise of trading centers. From 300 to 900 C.E.—the period that marks their golden era, the Classic Age—the Maya lived in a dozen densely packed city-states where astronomers charted planets, jewelers carved jade, and master builders constructed elaborate monuments, in which artists painted spectacular murals and carved stunning sculptures. Dates were chiseled across everything, in the numerical form dictated by the Long Count calendar, which during the Classic era was uniformly adopted.

Despite centuries of study, the Classic Maya still aren't fully understood. Their early civilization, the so-called Pre-Classic period from 2000 B.C. to 300 C.E., was typical for the time: Their early art consisted of unremarkable cave paintings and crude pots; their buildings were mostly thatched huts. Then, as if swept up in a cosmic create-a-thon, the Maya were suddenly energized and made a societal leap: They arose as skilled artists, engineers of intricate networks of irrigation, water storage, and canals, as well as master builders of precisely designed cities.

The Maya used dentists, who drilled and filled cavities—and filed teeth to points as fashion statements—while doctors tended to ills with medicines made of aloe and herbs. Their farming methods and irrigation systems were advanced. Commoners lived in adobe houses with gardens; kings and astronomer-shamans lived in palaces and four-sided pyramids with steep stairs to the top. Every city had at least one observatory, ball court, plaza, and temple, where high-drama ceremonies frequently unfolded; cities boasted hundreds of public buildings, all thick with sculptures and dotted with time-telling columns wrapped with chiseled dates.

The Maya invented their own stylized hieroglyphics and penned thousands of books on durable paper made from treated tree bark; they devised the world's most brilliant, and simple, numbering system, one that used only dots and bars—and in which the numbers five, thirteen, and twenty were believed to be powerfully charged. The Maya measured time with a dozen different calendars, which were used as fortune-telling devices and a means to predict eclipses or show when to declare war. Astrology was so key to the culture that it was built into the calendar—with the names of days and months factoring into the assessment. Holy men—who doubled as astronomers, astrologers, and calendar makers—held high rank, wrote books, and were awarded their own lavish pyramids as living quarters.

Keen astronomers and fervent students of the sciences of the day, the Maya were inconsistent in their understanding of the world. They attained a mind-boggling understanding of the heavens, but they also believed the world to be flat—or so it's deduced from their murals that show the disc held up on a tree. While they calculated the movements of the planets around the Earth, they apparently never caught on that the Earth revolved around the sun. They used the wheel—but only for toys—and these fierce warriors didn't rely on iron; their weapons were made of sharpened stone. They built ornate cities with the most primitive of tools.

Yet remarkable they were: Their ruins—in Palenque, Tikal, Copán, and beyond—leave permanent reminders that in their art, architecture, and engineering feats alone, the Maya were unusually advanced. Their marvels weren't for the faint of heart, however. Their rituals to celebrate and satiate their pantheon of deities were stirring and frequent: Human hearts were regularly ripped out on altars, fresh blood being required to keep the sun shining. Rulers tapped the wisdom of gods about matters from rain to war by pulling spiked ropes through their own tongues and piercing their privates with stingray spines.

For six centuries, the Mayan civilization was booming—with more and more lavish monuments rising; trade booming; more and more sculptures and murals appearing; books laden with history, esoteric, and planetary knowledge penned; and more and more Mayas employed as artisans and traders. But in the tenth century, the civilization of city-states crashed. Around 930 C.E., the Maya abruptly left most cities. The exodus, it now appears, was brought on by drought and famine—probably the result of local climate change, since by that time the Maya had chopped down all of the trees in their environment. From then on, the Maya civilization tumbled into irreversible decline.

A few outposts remained in the lowlands of the north, among them beautiful Chichén Itzá with its domed observatory, but the great civilization rapidly petered out as a new group—the militaristic and statue-building Toltecs, pushed out of northern Mexico by the fierce Aztecs—charged into Maya territory and scrambled to the top of the regional totem pole. By the time the Spanish conquistadors arrived in 1521, the Classic Maya were a blurry memory to everyone including most of their progeny. The Spanish conquistadors blotted their memory further. Most of the remaining Maya died from disease or the ensuing war; those who survived were subjected to further extermination, unless they embraced Catholicism. In what is now regarded as one of the greatest tragedies in the New World, the Spanish soon thereafter erased the local history and language in one fell swoop: They lit a bonfire and torched all Mayan books; the Maya's written hieroglyphs and their religion were banned.

For nearly one thousand years, the Maya were so thoroughly forgotten that even their millions of modern descendants knew little about them. The Classic Maya and their lost cities were rediscovered only two hundred years ago, when explorers hacked into jungles, opening this, and poking through that, releasing forgotten knowledge and sleeping spirits like genies.

The current remolding of the ancient Maya—as purveyors of doom—isn't the first time they have been misquoted, misrepresented, and miscast: The Maya civilization has often been misunderstood. No other civilization has inspired such outlandish theories and flights of fancy, which have sometimes taken on a life of their own. At least the initial confusion was understandable: The stunning remnants the Maya left were a tantalizing archeological striptease to nineteenth-century explorers; enthusiasts could project their fantasies, since there was no owner's manual to consult. Archeologists couldn't find a Mayan "Rosetta stone"—the multilingual dictionary that allowed archeologists to crack the Egyptian hieroglyphics—to provide clues to deciphering Mayan writing, a feat which after centuries of trying is still not entirely mastered.

Although Mayan hieroglyphics proved too daunting to read for most of two centuries, that didn't stop a plethora of scholars, writers, and enthusiasts from claiming to have cracked the code. In fact, it appears that a few cracked up while trying to unravel the hieroglyphic mystery and squeezing fantastical tales from the images—about arrivals from mythical lands or Maya conquests of Egypt, just a few of the ideas that have sent our understanding of the Maya astray. Even after two centuries of study, not all of the Maya's secrets have been revealed—but, nonetheless, the Maya have helped to drastically alter our world.

*Fig.05_* MAYAN HIEROGLYPHICS *Read top to bottom, two columns at a time, Maya hieroglyphics so stymied twentieth-century scholars that professors began sniffing that they were meaningless, little more than blocks of pretty graffiti to adorn buildings.*

THE INCIDENTAL CONQUEST

To understand the changes the Maya unleashed on modern humans—and how erroneous theories about them have rocked our world—it helps to trace their rediscovery.

Surprisingly, considering that they ruled over these parts for three hundred years, the Spanish had little to do with uncovering the ancient Maya culture, although they had plenty to do with stomping out the traces of the Maya world. Spain's lassoing of lands once ruled by the Maya wasn't planned, being a "while we are in the neighborhood, we might as well . . ." kind of conquest that was motivated by the search for riches and the desire to win converts to Christianity. Besides, it falsely appeared that the Yucatán peninsula, where the Maya were concentrated, would be easy to take over.

In 1521, when gold-seeking, Christianity-pushing Spaniards led by Hernán Cortés arrived in Central America, centuries of infighting and conquests by Toltecs and other rival civilizations had diluted the Mayan population, power, and territories. By the sixteenth century, most Maya lived in or near one coastal city, called Mérida by the Spanish. By then, memory of the brilliant if bizarre Mayan civilization that had once extended into Guatemala, southern Mexico, Honduras, Belize, and beyond, had grown hazy.

However, while they lacked intimate knowledge of the culture that preceded them, the early-sixteenth-century Maya still retained a good deal of the culture. They wrote in hieroglyphics, and some still spoke the language of their ancestors. They still put faith in shamans, followed a prophetic calendar of 260 days, worshipped many of the same gods, and retained the same creation myth—that the Maya had been formed from maize.

They still farmed, mined salt, retained a love of books, which they wrote out like the ancients on folded bark, and practiced ritual human sacrifice—the method of death for several of the earliest Spanish who accidentally sailed in to these parts.

The Spanish conquistadors who easily took Mexico City, capital of the Aztec people (who mistook Cortés for the returning god Quetzalcoatl, reported the Spanish), showed little interest in the former Maya land, once they discovered it was short on precious metals. The territory was handed over to Spanish priests; still in Inquisition mode, they proved themselves as capable of destruction as the greediest, most blood-thirsty warriors.

By the time Spaniards conquered the Yucatán peninsula, war and disease had wiped out 90 percent of the remaining Maya, but more were slaughtered during the act of conversion. Horrified by a religion that called for human sacrifices, the Spaniards forced survivors to embrace Christianity. In 1562, Spanish bishop Diego de Landa steamrolled a feared religious revival, burning all Mayan texts—some 10,000 books were torched in one day alone. He forced the Maya to adopt the Spanish language and banned all remaining vestiges of their culture—from writing hieroglyphics to using their calendars.

Perhaps out of guilt, de Landa also tried to record the culture with loving detail: His book *Relación de las cosas de Yucatán*—for centuries shelved in a convent in Madrid—listed customs, insights into the calendars, the Mayan alphabet, and the glyphs for dozens of names of days and months, although it was riddled with mistakes. Centuries later, his book would both help and hinder (because of its numerous errors) deciphering the world of the Maya that de Landa, more than any other, had helped destroy.

The discovery of the hidden Maya cities, crumbling and wrapped in vines, begins with the French, specifically the short, balding, and militarily skilled Napoléon Bonaparte. Snatching up lands from Spain to the Middle East, Napoléon created the conditions that would lead to the rediscovery of the Maya civilization. The first of Napoléon's two most important moves in that regard was conquering Egypt, a land then more rumored than known. Napoléon didn't simply send the navy to the land of pyramids in 1799; he assembled a shipload of France's finest minds and brightest stars to accompany him to the fabled land. So many members of France's intelligentsia—writers, botanists, architects, illustrators, engineers, linguists, philosophers, painters, and even a few poets—set sail to Egypt that some back home feared that France would lose her intellectual prowess should the ship sink.

Napoléon's investigating team did more than measure, draw, interview, analyze, and assess everything they could find in Egypt—from the hieroglyphic writing to the pyramids, the obelisks, the Sphinx, and local flora and fauna. They produced, among other things, the finest encyclopedia ever printed about the civilization along the Nile. They did more than uncover the Rosetta stone—a chiseled, cross-language lexicon that gave a Greek text alongside the Egyptian hieroglyphics, leading to their decipherment. And they did more than launch modern archeology by taking a multidisciplinary approach to understanding the past.

What Napoléon did with his Egyptian expedition—besides tick off the British, who soon sailed in to run the French out—was create a media frenzy, a new social fashion, a global fascination with antiquities and civilizations that had existed millennia before. As news, scientific reports, and fantastical illustrations of this exotic destination hit the world's printing presses, they inspired further exploration of worlds previously unknown and ignored. Europeans of all stripes—but above all the British—set out, picks and shovels in hand, digging up and documenting past civilizations in lands as far-flung as Mesopotamia and India.

Locales in the New World—particularly the land that trailed south from Mexico toward Panama—beckoned as well, but these territories were firmly locked up under Spanish control. Napoléon inadvertently remedied that situation as well. He lured Spanish king Carlos IV to France, where he tossed the monarch in prison. Then, in 1808, emperor Napoléon placed his heavily boozing brother Joseph on the Spanish throne. Roping Spain into the French empire was an ill-conceived political move that changed the face of the world. The Spanish loathed the drunken Frenchman, whom they nicknamed Pepe Bottellas—or "Joe Bottles"— and everyone from peasant farmer to plantation owner rose up against him. Most of Spain's armed forces sailed home to eject Joe Bottles during the Spanish War of Independence, which the Spaniards finally won in 1813.

But, the war against the French weakened Spain's hold over the colonies: When the troops were called home from the New World, locals organized rebellions against their colonial rulers. In 1821, the territories of Central America finally ran the Spanish out and declared independence.

The fantasies that still wrap the Maya began spinning from the first whack of an ax into the jungle that then choked much of Central America. Early European explorers were amazed as they cleared away vines, scraped off moss, and pulled away brush to expose the remains of once-elegant Mayan cities abandoned nearly a millennium before. Well, who could blame them? These cities were breathtaking. The meticulously ordered buildings, pyramids, and towers for stargazing—the highest in the Western Hemisphere—appeared to be of another world. Beautiful portraits of rulers wearing bird heads, stepped temples, palaces with courtyards and ball courts, and walls made of skulls amazed the explorers.

What these travelers uncovered was so mesmerizing, so astounding, and so mystifying that the enigmatic cities dominated academic circles and literate society. Throughout the 1800s, Europeans published hugely popular books on their finds, some filled mostly with drawings, others with glyphic writing so strange it might have been from a different planet.

Among the first to stumble upon the lost messages of the Maya was a wealthy eighteenth-century German, Alexander von Humboldt (1769–1859). Although he had no idea who had built the fine pyramids he uncovered in Mexico, his travels, his meticulous research, and his voluminous writings—printed as multi-volume encyclopedias—laid the foundation for understanding the forgotten civilization, which at that time didn't even have a known name.

ALEXANDER VON HUMBOLDT: THE EVOLUTION OF A DISCOVERY

A wealthy Prussian matron inadvertently financed the rediscovery of the Classic Maya civilization. In 1796, the mother of miner and geologist Alexander von Humboldt died in her hometown, Berlin, and von Humboldt suddenly found himself very rich. He came up with a rather novel idea—a scientific research trip to the New World that had no political objectives, a travel expedition that sought only to gather knowledge. The lands that most

*Fig.06*_CORTÉS CONQUERED THE WORLD VON HUMBOLDT
WOULD LATER INVESTIGATE

intrigued him in South and Central America, however, appeared impenetrable since they were firmly locked up by the colonial Spanish. Von Humboldt was undeterred. He was so enthusiastic about natural wonders and so fascinated by the secret natural treasures the Americas might hold that he convinced Spain's King Carlos IV to give him permission to explore. Accompanied by French botanist Aimé Jacques Alexandre Bonpland, von Humboldt set out in 1799 and became the first to carefully catalog flora, fauna, and monuments of Central and South America. His five years of travel so changed our understanding of the physical world that he is considered the father of geography at the least. Many hold him up as the one of the ancestors and finest minds of all science and natural history. Edgar Allan Poe dedicated his last work, *Eureka*, to von Humboldt; Thomas Jefferson proclaimed him the "most important scientist" whom the well-traveled and well-connected president had ever met; Charles Darwin called him a hero.

Mapping rivers, studying volcanoes, cataloguing thousands of plants, writing over sixty scientific volumes about his years trekking from Mexico to Peru, von Humboldt also planted the first seeds of interest in the Maya—whose civilization he erroneously confused with the Toltecs and Aztecs. As part of his well-received book *Vues des cordillères et monumens des peuples indigènes de l'Amerique*—or *Views of the cordilleras and monuments of the indigenous people of America*—he published a color plate showing five pages of the Dresden Codex, which kicked off a revolution of ideas.

Von Humboldt formulated theories that still hold today. For example, he made observations about the Earth's magnetic field, noting that it changed from poles to equator. He was the first to articulate the concept of continental drift and plate tectonics—the idea that all the continents formerly had been connected as one land mass. He also inspired the most radical idea of the nineteenth century. Von Humboldt's books about his observations, including species adaptation, deeply influenced traveling scientists Charles Darwin and Alfred Russel Wallace, whose studies of the natural world led them each to develop theories of evolution. Darwin's *On the Origin of Species* was published in 1859, just months after von Humboldt's death.

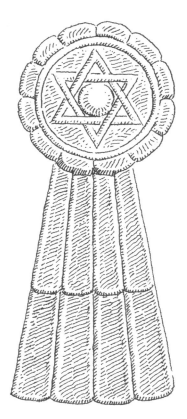

*Fig.07*_EARLY EXPLORERS EMBELLISHED THEIR DRAWINGS,
CREATING CONFUSION ABOUT THE ORIGINS OF THE MAYA

There in the midst of the jungle, von Humboldt and other explorers from the "civilized world" gazed at four-sided pyramids, observatories, temples, and tombs filled with jade and wrapped with hieroglyphs. The similarities with Egypt—pyramids and hieroglyphs—led explorers to make the first of many erroneous leaps of logic: These remarkable cities could only have been built by Egyptians. Never mind that the hieroglyphs weren't

Egyptian, the pyramids boasted steep flights of stairs, and the gods certainly weren't of the Egyptian pantheon. It was clear, they reported, that Egyptians had founded this civilization. To help make the case, illustrators brought in to record the finds added Egyptian touches to their drawings.

Scholars, at least some of them, scoffed at the notion of a mini-Egypt in the New World. The Egyptians weren't known for faraway journeys or colonizing, some said, so the idea was preposterous. Such splendorous cities must have been built by the ancient Greeks. Make that the Welsh or the Japanese. The bantering and debates grew loud and furious—making headline news, dominating discussions at cafés—as more and more eminent scholars and thinkers put in their two cents' worth. Few even considered that these secret cities and sacred sites might have been built by indigenous people. The descendants of the Maya were, after all, indigent farmers who seemed more likely to have been descendants of Leonardo da Vinci than of whoever had created these astounding buildings.

More explorers descended into the overgrown lands; more illustrators drew fantastical images, inserting elephants and adding Greek features to the people shown in drawings and sculptures. Printing presses across Europe cranked out travel books, art books, and encyclopedias documenting the antiquities of the "New World" and "proving" beyond all doubt that a civilization from elsewhere had built up these once-glorious cities. Even the publication of the entire Dresden Codex, widely circulated in 1825 as the third volume of the nine-volume *Antiquities of Mexico*, printed by British Lord Kingsborough—who died in debtors' prison crushed by the printer's bill from the venture—misrepresented the seventy-eight-page codex as a work of the Aztecs.

And the theories kept coming: The mysterious cities had been built by the Lost Tribes of Israel, Freemasons, Celtic Druids, seafaring Phoenicians, misplaced Polynesians, and/or a master race from a lost continent, who had stopped to build a few pyramids in ancient Egypt en route. Some pondered origins much farther away, speculating that the civilization had been built by visitors from Mars or planets far beyond. Their imaginative conclusions were understandable: The sites are physically stunning, and what's more, even diehard rationalists speak of these places as charged with a particularly intense energy. Even atheists whisper that it's as though spirits still lurk in these sites.

MAYAN ATTRACTIONS

PALENQUE (CHIAPAS, SOUTHERN MEXICO) Mystical Palenque, in the misty mountains of southern Mexico, is most famous as the seventh-century home of magician ruler Lord Pakal, one of the most powerful Maya and, to judge by his jade-filled tomb, one of the wealthiest. Palenque is spectacular, with a Palace complex—of four-story tower, interconnected buildings, and courtyards—several pyramid temples (including the hieroglyph-filled Temple of the Inscriptions), and an aqueduct. Hugely popular with tourists today, it served as jungle hotel for nineteenth-century explorers: Big names, from imaginative illustrator Jean-Frédéric Waldeck to photographer Alfred Maudslay, literally camped out in Palenque's crumbling temples for months at a time.

TIKAL (NORTHERN GUATEMALA) Accidentally uncovered by a manufacturer looking for gum trees in the mid-1800s, Tikal was once the most powerful city-state of the Maya civilization and

*Fig. 08_*TIKAL TEMPLE 1

home to more than 100,000 residents. It holds the tallest monuments of any Maya site—some pyramids shoot up 230 feet, higher than a twenty-story skyscraper—and the most monuments: Thousands of buildings once rose from the site that spread across 220 square miles. To date, only 10 square miles of the site have been fully excavated. Nine twin pyramid complexes, several acropolises, military fortifications, and magical gardens are just a few of the draws.

COPÁN (WESTERN HONDURAS) A trade city once famous for jade and obsidian, towering temples stacked upon older ones, and tunnels and tombs that lurked underneath, Copán stands out for its fabulous art, detailed portrait stelae of kings, and jaguar sculptures. Its Hieroglyphic Stairway is the oldest known example of Mayan hieroglyphics. Little more than root-wrapped ruins until the lost city was freed during excavations in the 1830s, Copán became world-famous after U.S. ambassador and travel writer John Lloyd Stephens wrote about it in the 1841 best-selling book *Incidents of Travel in Central America, Chiapas, and Yucatán*, for which Frederick Catherwood produced stunning illustrations.

UXMAL (YUCATÁN, MEXICO) Stunning architecture covered in stylized serpents and latticework is what makes this Yucatán site special. The names alone are compelling, ranging from the Pyramid of the Magician—a steep pyramid built over four others that shoots nearly 120 feet high—to the House of Turtles. The walled complex that the Spanish called the Palace of the Nuns belies its original purpose: It was a magicians' college for the Maya.

CHICHÉN ITZÁ (YUCATÁN, MEXICO) Settled by the Maya around 500 c.e., abandoned three centuries later, then resettled in 900, this site in the Yucatán is famous for the Pyramid of Kukulkan. During the spring and autumn equinoxes, a shadowed serpent appears to slither down the steep stairs of the pyramid. Each of four staircases to the central platform holds 91 steps, and the pyramid is considered a three-dimensional solar calendar; since the number of steps plus platform equal 365. The Toltecs conquered Chichén Itzá in 1000 c.e., and they are believed to have built its domed observatory, nicknamed "El Caracol" or "the Snail."

IZAPA (SOUTHEASTERN MEXICO) Hugging the Guatemalan border with southern Mexico, this site was originally settled by an earlier Mesoamerican civilization, the advanced Olmec— though some scholars believe it later became a Maya site. It is significant because the Olmec were the original developers of the Long Count calendar and perhaps the 260-day tzolkin as well.

Acclaimed scholar Vincent Malmstrom argues that the Long Count was developed here and was backdated to a day when the sun would have been at its highest at this location—August 13, 3114 B.C.E.—which would put the end date of the calendar at December 23, 2009. Writer John Major Jenkins disagrees, suggesting that the artwork and ball courts at Izapa give clues about what the end date is foretelling: "a rare alignment of the solstice sun with the Galactic Center"—a time he believes will trigger "tremendous transformation and opportunity for spiritual growth."[18]

Amid the wild theories that surrounded the discoveries of these jungle cities, two voices brought new insights. The first was that of amateur scientist Constantine Rafinesque, a Frenchman born in Turkey, who is now hailed as brilliant but was then known as an eccentric. A botanist, meteorologist, and name-giver of birds, he taught languages at Transylvania University in Kentucky, wrote books about Indian mounds in Ohio, and was forever going broke on get-rich-quick schemes. Rafinesque infuriated serious Maya scholars when he figured out two things that had been right under their noses. Studying the hieroglyphics in von Humboldt's *Views of the cordilleras* and the illustrations in the popular books of the day, Rafinesque was the first to conclude that the people who had written the Dresden Codex and built these cities weren't Aztecs, Toltecs, Egyptians, Phoenicians, or descendants of the Lost Tribes of Israel. Rafinesque was the first to assert that this writing came from the Classic Maya.

What's more, in 1832 Rafinesque wrote an article that provided the first inkling of what the codex was saying. Noting that nearly every drawing contained dots and bars—and that

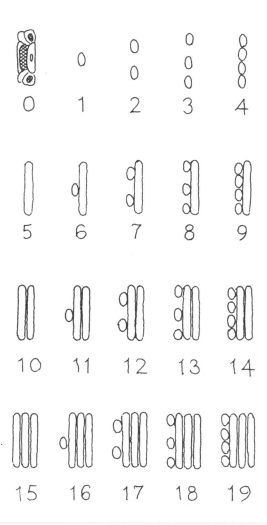

*Fig.09_* NUMBERS *Dots, bars, and shells (representing zero) are the only symbols used in the base-twenty Mayan number system. The Maya could write numbers in the dirt, pressing their fingers in for the dots and using the side of their hand for bars. Here, for instance, the numbers six and thirteen are added to yield nineteen.*

there were never more than four dots together—he deduced that each dot signified one, while a bar symbolized five. Although his findings weren't immediately embraced by all, he had indeed provided the first solid breakthrough in understanding the Mayan number system.[19]

Another leap was made when travel writer, author, and explorer John Lloyd Stephens turned his eye to the hills and swamps of this little-known region. Intrigued by the drawings from Central America, and believing that some of the images were unreliable, he began planning a journey with well-known British architect-illustrator Frederick Catherwood to shed light on the jungle-covered secrets.

[In Copán, Honduras] we returned to the base of the pyramidal structure, and ascended by regular stone steps, in some places forced apart by bushes and saplings, and in others thrown down by the growth of large trees . . . In parts they were ornamented with sculptured figures and rows of death's heads. Climbing over the ruined top, we reached a terrace overgrown with trees . . . we ascertained to be a square, and with steps on all the sides almost as perfect as those of the Roman amphitheatre. The steps were ornamented with sculpture, and on the south side . . . was a colossal head, evidently a portrait . . .

[We] strove in vain to penetrate the mystery by which we were surrounded. Who were the people that built this city? . . . America, say historians, was peopled by savages; but savages never reared these structures, savages never carved these stones . . . [A]rchitecture, sculpture, and painting, all the arts which embellish life, had flourished in this overgrown forest; orators, warriors, and statesmen, beauty, ambition, and glory, had lived and passed away, and none knew that such things had been, or could tell of their past existence. Books, the records of

knowledge, are silent on this theme. The city was desolate. No remnant of this race hangs round the ruins, with traditions handed down from father to son, and from generation to generation . . . none to tell whence she came, or what caused her destruction; . . . The place where we sat, was it a citadel from which an unknown people had sounded the trumpet of war or a temple for the worship of the God of peace or did the inhabitants worship the idols made with their own hands, and offer sacrifices on the stones before them? All was mystery, dark, impenetrable mystery, and every circumstance increased it.

In Egypt the colossal skeletons of gigantic temples stand in the unwatered sands in all the nakedness of desolation; here an immense forest shrouded the ruins, hiding them from sight, heightening the impression and moral effect, and giving an intensity and almost wildness to the interest.[20]

Well-connected in political circles, Stephens was appointed by President Martin Van Buren as special ambassador to Central America, a title which helped facilitate his treks up mountains, through forests, and across bogs—from Honduras to the Yucatán. The reports that resulted from the explorations of Stephens and illustrator Catherwood were a turning point: These two men were the first to realistically document what they found. Catherwood's illustrations were gorgeous, Stephens's writing was inspired, and their resulting two-volume book further stirred up awe and romantic yearnings about the former inhabitants of the New World. While he couldn't believe that the Maya had created these architectural masterpieces—the local peoples, nineteenth-century Maya, when asked about who had lived in these cities, had shrugged "Who knows?"—Stephens was the first to assert authoritatively that whoever had built these pyramids and temples must have been homegrown.

*Fig. 10_* MORE THAN MERE ORNAMENTATION. SCULPTURES
HAD DATES CHISELED ON THEIR SIDES.

HOW THE MAYA CREATED THE PANAMA CANAL

Stephens's travels were remarkable in another way: His fascination with the Maya, while passionate and sincere, covered up another agenda. Stephens was a spy.

The appointment by President Van Buren of Stephens as special ambassador to Central America was a cover: Stephens was scarcely an ambassador in the formal sit-in-the-office-and-shake-hands-with-dignitaries sense of the word. Van Buren had sent him off with a secret mission: to assess the possibility of building a canal across Panama that would link Pacific and Atlantic, a project that Van Buren wanted Stephens to negotiate. The traveler-ambassador reported back that, while indeed the creation of such a canal was feasible, the political climate didn't favor it: Wars were breaking out across the newly independent territories, including in Colombia, from which Panama was attempting to break away.

However, Stephens—encouraged by the president and financed by New York industrialists—struck another deal: He made a successful bid to build the Panama Railroad, soon becoming president of the venture. The endeavor was the first significant move by North Americans into the lands to the south, and it facilitated not only the independence of Panama from Colombia but also the building of the Panama Canal, which opened in 1913. What's more, the Panama Railroad Company opened the door to similar moves elsewhere. The Costa Rica Rail Company ultimately became the banana-growing United Fruit Company, which turned Costa Rica and Guatemala into unstable and poverty-ridden "banana republics," where American business often played a heavy hand in local politics. This was most clearly illustrated in 1954, when the Central Intelligence Agency (CIA) orchestrated the overthrow of the democratically elected president of Guatemala Jacobo Árbenz, whose land reform programs were deemed threatening to U.S.-owned banana companies.[21] The first step onto this slippery slope had been made by John Stephens, brought to the region initially simply by his fascination with the disappeared Mayan cities.

Stephens's explorations illustrated two other realities—the Maya had forgotten the ancients, and when it came to the public, reality didn't particularly matter.

Wowed by the ruins of Copán and hoping to purchase artifacts for the National Museum in Washington, D.C., the diplomat-explorer met with the owner of the land and ended up purchasing the city—for a mere 50 dollars, an amount that reflects how disconnected from the ancient Maya the locals had become.

The other truth his visit demonstrated was one that still haunts this arena today: namely, that when it comes to the Maya, the truth doesn't really matter. Even though Stephens's book was a best-seller—Edgar Allan Poe called it "perhaps the most interesting book of travel ever published"—his realism didn't halt the sensationalism and strange, seemingly unfounded, ideas about the Maya, which continued flooding the media through the nineteenth century and haven't stopped today. Whether for reasons of religion, ego, commerce, or even psychosis, the solid facts about the Maya have for centuries now been twisted, distorted, and clouded.

CLOUDING THE ISSUES

The arena of the Maya has often been a battleground for agendas and egos, fights that have obscured the search for truth about this Mesoamerican civilization. A few historical agendas to note:

THE MORMON CHURCH Joseph Smith, founder of the Mormon Church, was eager to link these new discoveries with the lost tribes of Israel. The idea of portraying the New World as the New Zion—a land for God's chosen people—formed a basis for his new religion. Following Smith's example, the Church of Jesus Christ of Latter-Day Saints has funded numerous explorations to Central America, apparently with an eye to making that link. In fact, Brigham Young University in Utah is now one of the world's finest archeology schools. While non-Mormon scholars applaud the work and reports of those graduating from this program, they note that it is believed that Mormon archeologists submit rather different reports to the Mormon elders than they do to other academics. They also caution that any claims about the "Mayan prophecies" from scholars and archeologists may well be linked to the religious beliefs of those making the claim.

DOUBLE AGENTS Many explorers, like Stephens himself, had political and economic motives up their sleeves, secretly serving as spies who mapped terrain and assessed development pos-sibilities, vulnerabilities, and political leanings in the lands recently freed from Spain. Both the United States and France sent their militaries into Mesoamerica during the nineteenth century. Between 1846 and 1848, the United States fought Mexico in the war that broke out after the United States annexed Texas; in 1862, France launched a five-year military attempt to permanently pocket Mexico in its colonial suit. The issue of spy-explorers stirred controversy well into the twentieth century: archeologist Sylvanus Morley, who excavated Chichén Itzá for the Carnegie Institution and Copán for Harvard's Peabody Museum (which got half of Copán's unearthed treasures in return), was also accused of being a spook by contemporaries—a claim later proven true. The Department of Naval Intelligence paid him to snoop on Germans and keep an eye on American economic interests such as United Fruit. Such political and economic agendas continually colored what were submitted to the public as unbiased journalistic reports and scholarly studies.

ACADEMIC SHOWDOWNS Through the nineteenth and twentieth centuries, scholarly duels frequently broke out over the facts about the Maya, who have inadvertently ruined many a scholarly career. Powerful archeologist Eric S. Thompson, employed by the Carnegie Institution and Field Museum of Natural History in Chicago, and Carnegie's Sylvanus Morley were two who held back understanding. They both insisted, for example, that the Mayan language couldn't be spoken, and they steamrolled the careers of those who thought otherwise, including Russian scholar Yuri Knorozov. Progress in deciphering the language was nearly halted, as we shall see, on several occasions, simply because a respected scholar decreed what the truth was, often enough being entirely wrong. Given the ideological knockouts over the Maya that have raged for centuries, it's surprising that we have many facts to work with at all: The greatest leaps in understanding the Maya have been made only in the past thirty years.

ARMAGEDDON The ancient Maya are continually yanked out as "prophets" by any number of groups who need doomsayers (who can't talk) to make their case. Some evangelical Christians point to the termination of the Long Count calendar as just more proof that we're approaching the End Times and the battle of Armageddon. Others, apparently hoping to spur awareness about issues such as climate change or promote their product, are hooking their cause to 2012's star, embracing the turnover date of the Long Count calendar simply as a publicity tool. The movie *2012*, for example, initially had nothing to do with the Maya—nor was it called *2012*. It was planned as a movie about a "second Noah's Ark" says director-producer Roland Emmerich. Along the way, his coproducer noticed the 2012 craze—and they decided to weave in the "social movement" as a prominent feature of the movie.

The reason we've been smacked with so many "untruths" about the Maya isn't simply that some people have had agendas to further: The Maya have also had a bizarre effect on those who study them. Many who have trod into this field appear to have been "touched" by Maya mania—particularly once they set eyes on the hieroglyphs. It's not an exaggeration to say that more than any other culture in history the Maya have driven those who study them goofy.

"I've never known of another culture," says professor David Stuart, "that has prompted more people to claim that its inhabitants came from outer space."[22]

Take the case of popular nineteenth-century archeologist and photographer Augustus Le Plongeon. He announced that he'd deciphered a tomb inscription telling that a broken heart had prompted Mayan Queen Moo to sail off to rule over Egypt, and he added that Queen Moo had been his wife in a past life. More recently, writer Erich von Däniken launched the idea that the Maya (and other ancients) were space travelers with his best-selling book *Chariots of the Gods?* Art historian José Argüelles, PhD, keeps insisting that not only were the ancients actually galactic agents from far-off orbs but that, come December 2012, we'll be having a galactic reunion with our neighbors.

But no one fell harder and indirectly steered humanity on a more dangerous course by his battiness than nineteenth-century Flemish priest C. E. Brasseur de Bourbourg. Able to access church vaults and cobwebbed libraries in Madrid, Brasseur was a treasure seeker. His early contributions were astounding: Brasseur had a knack for uncovering valuable writings, among them the *Popol Vuh*, an encyclopedia of Mayan myths and history, that had been hidden in a church altar—a book that he translated and had published in 1841. He dug up Diego de Landa's dusty manuscript, *Relación de las cosas de Yucatán*, which provided insights into the pre-Christian Maya culture and also lists the names of glyphs. Brasseur also translated and published de Landa's work two years later. But when he came across one of the old Mayan books written by a thirteenth-century shaman, he went over the edge.

Believing he had broken the hieroglyphic code, even though he was reading his codex backwards, Brasseur began ranting about an idea that hadn't been much talked about since the ancient Greeks. He insisted that the hieroglyphs told the story of an escape from a sunken land mass, and concluded that the Maya's ancestors were actually escapees from the lost continent of Atlantis—a mythical island first publicized by Plato in 360 B.C.E. and mostly forgotten. Scholars scoffed, but Brasseur struck a popular note with this Atlantis idea, not knowing that his writings would set off a chain of events that would help launch World War II.

HOW LOVE OF THE MAYA LED TO THE NAZIS

A mythical land little known before Brasseur started flapping his jaw about it, Atlantis became the rage of the late 1800s. It was adopted as a theme for Mardi Gras and costume parties, and it inspired the publication of a number of maps showing its location, as well as that of another lost continent, Mu. In 1882, former U.S. Senator Ignatius Donnelly grew so inspired by Brasseur's idea that he wrote a best-selling book about Atlantis that permanently stamped the concept of a lost continent into popular culture.

But a stout Russian mystic with swirling eyes—Madame Helena Blavatsky—who cofounded the influential Theosophical Society in New York, took the idea of the lost continent one dangerous step further. In her book, *Isis Unveiled*, published in the midst of the Atlantean craze, she popularized the notion that the lost continent had been home to a master race of people: the Aryans.

Some Aryans, she asserted, set up the Mayan empire, others headed to Egypt, India, and the Holy Land near Jerusalem. Widely read in the late 1800s—particularly by those who joined her mystical and controversial Theosophical Society—her occult books about this superior Aryan race, including *The Secret Doctrine*, were devoured several decades later by an Austrian living in Germany, Adolf Hitler. In short, spinning off of the Maya mania and the subsequent Atlantis revival, occultist Madame Blavatsky planted the idea of this Aryan superrace in Hitler's head. And while he changed their looks—the Aryans described by Blavatsky were dark-haired and swarthy skinned—Hitler embraced her idea, making it a key element of his Nazi society. The Führer was apparently so moved by her books that he snagged one of the two Theosophical Society symbols—the swastika. The other symbol used by the society and stamped on every book alongside the swastika also showed up in Hitler's world, though it was cast in a different light—the Star of David.

While odd theories were spinning in stormy directions, a few more leaps were made in understanding the Maya. In 1880, German librarian Ernst Förstemann broke part of the hieroglyphic code: He deciphered astronomical notations in the Dresden Codex—working out tables tracing the movements of Venus and the moon. What's more, he unraveled the meaning of numbers that ran in columns alongside ribbons of glyphs. They were calendars. Förstemann was so intrigued that he too published copies of the Dresden Codex so others could study it, and his version was by far the most accurate—giving scholars worldwide their best shot so far at understanding the Classic Maya, a civilization that was absorbed with time.

Beyond the practical aspects of keeping track of days, the Classic Maya regarded the measurement of time as a mystical endeavor that married magic, stargazing, religion, and powerful cosmic forces. The activity was regarded as so metaphysical that certain VIP shamans were tapped as official "day keepers" who charted the passage of days according to various cycles—some lasting nine months, some stretching half a century, some viewing time over several millennia. These unusual calendars showcased the civilization's fascination with numbers, their devotion to astrology, their worship of gods—and their love of combining elements to create something new. They also high-lighted the idea that time was cyclical.

The Maya believed that certain numbers were particularly potent; they viewed planets as so influential upon daily life that they tallied the celestial movements in assorted calendars, some tracking the moon, some following Venus, some tracing the movement of the sun, and some combining the passing of all the heavenly bodies. They also gave homage to the deities by naming days and months of these assorted calendars after their many gods. And they viewed calendar dates—which com-bined numbers, star positions, and god names—as auguries.

TIME MATTERS

Besides giving us the willies about our future, the Classic Maya have induced a global migraine, as modern humans try to understand their elegant but complex time system involving particularly charged numbers, wheels, dots, bars, and dozens of god names affixed to days and months.

In fact, the Maya used several calendars. Among the most important:

THE TZOLKIN The holy 260-day calendar—still used by some modern Maya—was used to chart pregnancies and was heavily relied on for its predictive qualities. It ran a cycle of thirteen num-bers against twenty days with names drawn from gods, such as Imix (crocodile), Ik (wind), Akbal (jaguar), and Kan (maize). The days are numbered 1 through 13 (each number having a certain quality) and cycled through the named days (also with ascribed characteristics) like two gears meshing. Thus over 260 days the tzolkin can be counted in the following way: 1 Imix, 2 Ik, 3 Akbal, 4 Kan, 5 Chicchan, 6 Cimi, 7 Manik, 8 Lamat, 9 Muluc, 10 Oc, 11 Chuen, 12 Eb, 13 Ben (note that the numbers begin repeating here, while the twenty names are still changing) 1 Ix, 2 Men, 3 Cib, 4 Cabab, 5 Eznab, 6 Cauac, 7 Ahau (note that here the day names are repeating, while the numbers continue) 8 Imix, 9 Ik . . .

THE HAAB The 365-day solar calendar guided planting—it is actually made up of twenty named "months" of 18 days each, with 5 days, considered unlucky, tacked on at the end. It is counted in a similar way to the Gregorian calendar: Each month is numbered with 20 days—0 through 19. Thus the month of Pop begins with Pop 0, then Pop 1 and Pop 2. Month names in the haab are also derived from gods, of which the Maya clearly had many: Pop, Uo, Zip, Zotz, Tzec, Xul, Yaxkin, Mol, Chen, Yax, Zac, Ceh, Mac, Kankin, Muan, Pax, Kayab, and Cumbku to be specific. Each month has a certain characteristic, which is intensified or minimized by the number of the date.

THE FIFTY-TWO-YEAR CALENDAR ROUND This calendar charts the tzolkin and haab together (see the illustration on page 83) to give detailed astrological and astronomical forecasts and yields dates such as 8 Imix, 13 Pop—the 8 Imix marking the day in the tzolkin calendar against the 13 Pop of the haab calendar.

THE LONG COUNT CALENDAR Used during the Classic era, this calendar covers 5,125.34 years and allowed the Maya to calculate and predict eclipses, transits of Venus, and other celestial activities thousands of years into the past and future. It is typically written in numerical form, like an odometer. It measures (from smallest to largest):

> Kins—or days—written from 1 to 19
>
> Uinals—or months of 20 days—written from 1 to 18
>
> Tuns—years of 360 days—written from 1 to 19
>
> Katuns (roughly 20 years)—written from 1 to 19
>
> Baktuns (roughly 394 years)—written from 1 to 13

The period of 5,125 years that coincides with the ending of thirteen baktuns in the Long Count calendar is also counted as a Great Cycle—one-fifth of the "Grand Cycle" of nearly 26,000 years, the length of time Mesoamericans believed humanity had existed. John Major Jenkins and others point out that 26,000 years is also the amount of time it takes for the earth to fully complete

*Fig.11_*HOW TIME WORKED ACCORDING TO THE MAYA (CALENDAR ROUND, HAAB AND TZOLKIN COMBINED) *The sacred 260-day tzolkin calendar, created by multiplying the powerful numbers thirteen and twenty, highlighted ceremonial days. The 365-day calendar called the haab was designed for agriculture, showing the planting seasons and planetary movements during the solar year. For more precise information about the nature of each day, these two calendars were "spun" against each other in the calendar wheel. Providing an in-depth horoscope and numerology reading, the calendar wheel was the ultimate "fortune-telling" device, favoring some activities and boding ill for others, depending on how the stars, numbers, and god names lined up.*

However, the time frame of this calendar wheel was short: Every fifty-two years, the same exact dates repeated again, leading to confusion, for example, in tracing the history of a dynastic rule. To stretch the amount of time covered, while still paying attention to the special character of each day, the Maya "anchored" the wheel against a calendar that spanned a much longer period time. They "spun" the wheel along the Long Count calendar, which stretched over five thousand years (not pictured). The illustration to the right gives an idea about how time rolled along to form the calendar wheel. (See "Time Matters," page 80.)

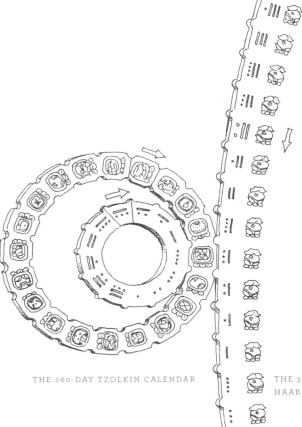

THE 260-DAY TZOLKIN CALENDAR

THE 365-DAY
HAAB CALENDAR

"the precession of the equinoxes"—the westward motion of the equinoxes and the shift of the North Star that occurs because of Earth's tilt as it makes its yearly revolutions around the same point. And this is considered significant astrologically—and, says Jenkins, astronomically—because it places the Earth in alignment with the sun and the center of the Milky Way in the year 2012.

The Mayan Long Count calendar covers such a vast stretch of time that no physical example has ever been found; scholars doubt that a physical representation was actually used by the ancients. The huge stone disc with the sun in the middle that the History Channel is so fond of showing is actually an Aztec calendar, not a Long Count calendar, which the Aztec didn't use.

In short, the Mayan Long Count calendar isn't a tangible thing. It's just a working theory—an elegant system, say its proponents, to tell time thousands of years ahead or back. For centuries, the calendars were nearly all we understood about the Maya. The notion that the Maya were time obsessed, says David Stuart, reflects the lack of genuine leaps in understanding for most of the two centuries they've been under modern humans' microscope. Anthropologists, archaeologists, linguists, and heads of esteemed institutions like Harvard, the Carnegie Institution, and Yale, after devoting their entire careers to studying the Maya, had until recently really only graduated to the Mayan equivalent of kindergarten: They could count and tell time.

Once their calendar system had been worked out by contemporary scholars, a crucial question remained: What were the starting and ending dates of the calendar? The answers to those questions kicked off a whole new round of questioning and wild theorizing, and that should not come as a surprise. Only one thing can be counted on with the Maya: To judge from recent centuries, wherever stories about the Maya go, you can be sure that illogical leaps of thought, controversial theories, and occasional brilliant insights will follow. In the course of unraveling the meaning of the Maya's cryptograms and image-studded languages, wild theories and far-out speculations have sprouted, and continue to sprout, like mushrooms in a cow patch. The Maya still aren't fully understood, but scholars have made astounding leaps in recent decades. Alas, as we shall see, the scholars are mostly being ignored, as a school of hallucinating modern shamans has yanked control of the Maya and is spewing out ideas that have little resemblance to fact. More talked about than ever, the Maya are, more than ever, misunderstood.

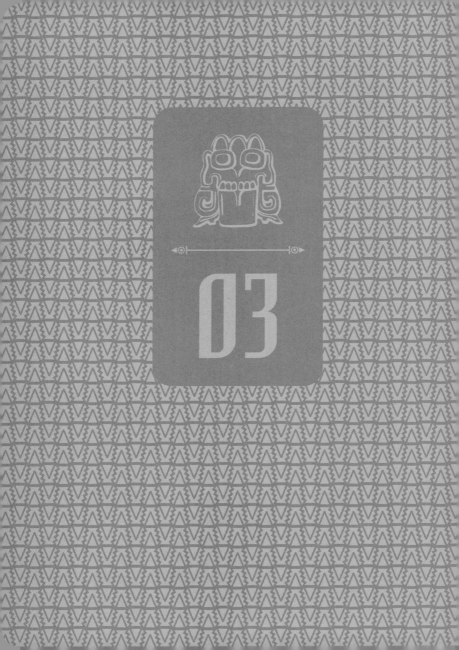

03

MODERN
MYTH
MAKERS

Seers, Shamans, Spinners, and Dream Weavers

When J. W. Goodman (California gold prospector, publisher, playwright, author, amateur anthropologist, vineyard owner, and the newspaper editor who first hired Mark Twain) sat down to solve a particularly difficult puzzle at the turn of the twentieth century, he had no idea that he would trigger global panic a century later. An aficionado of puzzles ever since Edgar Allan Poe had kicked off a cryptogram craze, the dapper intellectual didn't know that the code he was deciphering would reveal a date that would later be infamous as a day of global doom. He would have fallen off his chair laughing if he'd realized that the information he was about to hand over to humanity would be tied up with "galactic beams" and would have future writers dropping hallucinogens to gain insights from insects. In fact, given the chilly response to Goodman's announcement when he solved the puzzle—figuring out how to correlate the Mayan calendar to ours—it seemed highly unlikely that his decipherment would be recalled at all.

Goodman's 1905 findings didn't rock the world. They didn't make even the back pages of the widely read publications of the day. For nearly fifty years, Goodman's "discovery" elicited only snickers from scholars, who scoffed at the idea that an amateur could unlock one of the biggest Mayan riddles that had eluded the fine minds of Yale, Harvard, and the Carnegie Institution, who'd been pondering that same puzzle for decades. Being unable to correlate the Maya date to our calendar had proved a roadblock to further studies. After all, a calendar dating a lost civilization—even if beautifully chiseled on temples and tombs—isn't all that useful if you can't tie it to a modern timekeeping system. The information provided by the Long Count was baffling, on par with asking the time of day and being told, "It's precisely 33,000 after 82 million." Goodman's short article, which appeared in the issue of *Anthropology Today* in 1905, did indeed solve the mystery of converting the Mayan calendar. By tying a date in that calendar to the Gregorian calendar, he allowed calculation of both a beginning date and an end date of the Long Count—the timekeeping device to which more fantasies have now been pinned than a *Playboy* calendar.

*Fig.12*_LORD PAKAL'S SARCOPHAGUS *The tomb of seventh-century Maya king Lord Pakal, discovered in Palenque's Temple of the Inscriptions in 1952, held such astounding wealth that it reignited interest in the Maya, launching yet more fanciful tales. Some believed that the bas-relief of Pakal proved that he was a space traveler, his hands working the controls of a space ship. Decades after his tomb was opened, Pakal uttered warnings, prophecies, and calendar tips—via a West Coast–based art history professor named José Argüelles.*

Even when the calendar's start date (believed to be August 11, 3114 B.C.E.) and "turnover date" (December 21, 2012) was finally agreed upon in the 1950s, the news scarcely jolted the world, barely even rippling in academia. No headlines trumpeted, "World to End in 2012!" No magazine, no newspaper, no journals, and no books immediately associated it with doomsday. Few publications back then even mentioned that scholars had finally agreed on the date—well, as much as scholars ever agree on anything. By then, for the first time, the Maya were simmering on the back burner. Issues like World War II, communism, nuclear war, UFOs, FDR, and JFK had clouded over interest in jungle mysteries. Until, that is, a Mexican archeologist yanked on a stone—and discovered that it opened a secret tomb.

In the mosquito-thick jungle of Mexico in 1952, the surprise discovery of a tomb holding Palenque King Lord Pakal (ruled 615–683 C.E.) rekindled the mystery of the Maya and ultimately led to what many scholars regard as some of the biggest whoppers being told about the lost civilization and 2012. Believed to be a powerful magician, and without question the mightiest Mayan leader of his day, Lord Pakal lived for eighty years, built irrigation and water storage projects, conquered nearby city-states, commissioned many of the civilization's most stunning monuments and elegant sculptures, and was worshipped as a demigod until his death, when the demi was dropped and he ascended to full-fledged god status.

LORD PAKAL, REIGNITER OF THE MAYA FLAME

The holes bothered him. In the late 1940s, Alberto Ruz Lhuillier, director of research for Mexico's Instituto Nacional de Arqueología e Historia, noticed a row of holes in a stone slab at the top of Palenque's highest pyramid, the Temple of the Inscriptions. The holes in this temple, which bore more hieroglyphic inscriptions than any other yet uncovered, must signify that the stone could be hoisted, he insisted. In spite of his colleagues' incredulity, he believed that below the slab lay a tomb—a conclusion that baffled others, since no Mayan pyramids had been known to serve as burial spots. But when he and his workers lifted the slab, they found a stairway below filled with rubble, that descended to a network of hidden rooms above a secret chamber.

*Fig.13_*ARCHEOLOGIST ALBERTO RUZ LHUILLIER
KICKED OFF A MAYA REVIVAL

"Out of the dim shadows," Ruz later wrote, "emerged a vision from a fairy tale, a fantastic, ethereal sight from another world. It seemed a huge magic grotto carved out of ice, the walls sparkling and glistening like snow crystals. Delicate festoons of stalactites hung like tassels of a curtain, and the stalagmites on the floor looked like drippings from a great candle. The impression, in fact, was that of an abandoned chapel. Across the walls marched stucco figures in low relief. Then my eyes sought the floor. This was almost entirely filled with a great carved stone slab, in perfect condition."[23] What he described was the lid of a remarkable sarcophagus, painted with a mercurial substance that even a thousand years later was so deadly it would have killed those who touched it. (The ornate sarcophagus lid, apparently showing Pakal heading off to the underworld, was a cause of wonderment—and more Mayan fantasies of the modern kind. The carved lid led Danish author Erich von Däniken to launch his idea about galaxy-touring Maya-nauts.)

Ruz had uncovered the most spectacular archeological find in Mesoamerica—the tomb of Lord Pakal, ruler of Palenque. Jade ornaments spilled out of the tomb; the king wore jade jewelry around his neck and hanging from his ears and held jade figurines in his hands. A dramatic jade mask covered his face. In death and beyond he was watched over by six guards, whose skeletons were found alongside his sarcophagus. Covered with dates, the last being 692—apparently the year of his burial—the tomb itself provided more mysteries: The body inside was initially believed to be that of a forty-year-old man, although Pakal had died at age eighty. Debate about exactly who lay in the tomb still lingers, some wondering if Pakal had already passed and a double filled in for the last years of his reign, or if he had just aged remarkably well. The appearance of icy stalagmites in the bowels of the temple were unusual, some believed, given that this was a tropical zone. And some say that, when the tomb was opened, Ruz spoke of hearing voices and feeling a procession of spirits passing by.

What is clear: Ruz opened a Pandora's box when he lifted the stone. Some 2012 promoters have pried open Lord Pakal's mouth like that of a marionette, and they've filled it with words of questionable credibility, making the dead man a leading source for a "Maya prophecy" as well as an advocate for a special lunar calendar—a timekeeping device that isn't even Mayan, but actually and conveniently is the creation of the man who claims to have given voice to dead Lord Pakal—José Argüelles.

The 1952 discovery of Lord Pakal's tomb relit interest in the Maya, although back then few were thinking of 2012. The murmurings of a calamitous future didn't surface until the '60s and '70s. The seed idea of 2012 came from several sources: a respected scholar (spreading a rumor), a respected Lakota Indian poet (spreading a prophecy), and a respected spiritual author (interweaving legends of assorted Indian tribes into a call for a leap into the Age of Aquarius). From there, schemers, trippers, and madmen have jumped in along with scientific writers, scientists, and linguists—to put forth a kaleidoscope of possibilities, many of them quite hard to prove. Here is the short list of early 2012 publishing:

THE MAYA by Michael Coe The idea that the Maya believed that when the Long Count rolled over to 13.0.0.0.0 civilization would simultaneously roll over and play dead started, it appears, with esteemed Yale anthropologist Michael Coe, who colleagues say is now red-faced that he played any role in what would become 2012 madness. In the 1966 edition of his book *The Maya*, he wrote, "There is a suggestion . . . that Armageddon would overtake the degenerate peoples of the world and all creation on the final day of the thirteenth [baktun]. Thus . . . our present universe . . . [would] be annihilated . . . when the Great Cycle of the Long Count reaches completion." Coe has deleted this observation from subsequent printings of the book and has reportedly confessed to colleagues that he threw the idea in only as a bit of color.

CHARIOTS OF THE GODS? by Erich von Däniken Two years after the publication of Coe's book, Danish hotelkeeper Erich von Däniken speculated in his 1968 book, *Chariots of the Gods?* that the Maya came from outer space. The sarcophagus lid of Lord Pakal's tomb was proof, said the Dane, as it showed that the Maya king was an astronaut.

MEXICO MYSTIQUE by Frank Waters Weaving together threads of myth and legends from the Hopi, Aztec, and Maya, in 1971 mystical writer Frank Waters pointed to the end of the Maya calendar as a sendoff point when we can enter the "sixth dimension" and the Age of Aquarius.

LORD OF THE DAWN by Tony Shearer Published the same year as Waters's book, Shearer's attributed a "prophecy poem" to the Aztec feathered serpent god Quetzalcoatl. Shearer reported that, before disappearing, Quetzalcoatl prophesied periods of "thirteen Heavens and nine Hells" each lasting fifty-two years. According to Shearer, the final hell would end on August 16, 1987, a potentially dangerous day that, should it be survived, would culminate in an era of peace. When Shearer passed his idea on to an art historian teaching at the University of Colorado, it would help kick off the 2012 phenomenon swirling today—since it would jump-start the New Age phenomenon that helped make it all possible—with the launch of the Harmonic Convergence. (See page 104.)

Further aiding the planting of misinformation and half-baked ideas about 2012 was the slow progress in translating hieroglyphics, which into the 1970s still had scholars scratching their heads. Some at the time were tempted to assume that hidden in the glyphs was confirmation of their ideas about "ancient Maya prophecies" concerning the end of the world. A few decades ago, however, sudden jumps were made; in the past thirty years, most hieroglyphs have been translated. It turns out that the Maya weren't very concerned with what might go down more than a thousand years later. The hieroglyphics negate the idea that the Maya predicted a cataclysmic end.

CODE CRACKERS

By the mid-twentieth century, after long decades of knocking their heads against the wall, scholars had pretty much given up on deciphering the exacts of Mayan hieroglyphs. Leading Maya experts kept stressing the numbers and calendars, while downplaying the writing, insisting that the language of the ancient Maya couldn't be spoken, that it was nonsensical artwork, or that, whatever it was, this monument-wrapping graffiti simply didn't matter.

Ever since they were first shown to the world, Mayan hieroglyphics proved a gnarly puzzle. The initial problem was not being able to clearly see what was chiseled and painted: early illustrators, after all, had a tendency to draw what they fancied, embellishing the reality with icons from other cultures. In the 1880s, two things brought the images into sharper focus: Diplomat-photographer Alfred Maudslay hauled thousands of pounds of camera equipment up mountains and into dense brush to record the glyphs more precisely, and Förstemann published a more

detailed printing of the Dresden Codex. Despite the improve-
ments, little progress was made in understanding what the
hieroglyphs revealed. In the 1930s, heavyweight archeologist and
linguist Eric Thompson devised a new method of grouping the
glyphs, but he insisted they represented only ideas, not sounds.
His interpretation was countered by Soviet linguists and anthropologists, but their protests were quashed.

*Fig. 14*_GRAD STUDENT LINDA SCHELE
AND TEEN DAVID STUART

According to Michael Coe, who documents the decipherment
in his book *Breaking the Maya Code*, the first big step was taken
in the 1970s: American grad student Linda Schele and Austra-
lian grad student Peter Mathews, while at a seminar in Mexico,
realized that much of the Maya writing concerned family trees.
Rulers weren't making grand predictions—they were detailing
their personal histories. Testing their theory on one monument,
they quickly stitched together much of the history of Palenque.
The grad students blew away the old masters in deciphering
the meaning of characters, but a decade later a teenager went
even further. In 1981, fifteen-year-old David Stuart, son of Mayan

archeologists, presented an academic paper that proved that the Maya language was indeed spoken. The teenager demonstrated how Mayan writers played word games—substituting differ-ent glyphs for the same sounds—the same way we might write *fone* for *phone*. His finding allows most of the Mayan writing to be finally understood as a spoken tongue.

But, even with the hieroglyphic code cracked, all the answers aren't in. Rain has washed away key glyphs in inscriptions, wind has eroded stone faces, walls have crumbled, paint has chipped, fires have torched wooden beams, pages have ripped and crum-bled to dust. And even with many pieces assembled, there's still debate on what the Maya intended. Nevertheless, they didn't seem to have much to say about the end of the calendar. Monu-ment 6, a stone in Tortuguero, Mexico, a relatively insignificant city in Tabasco, is the only bit of ancient Maya writing that men-tions the 2012 date at all, and most of the glyphs on it are unde-cipherable. The message it imparts, which has become the basis for the 2012 panic: "The thirteenth pik [baktun] will be finished [on] Four Ahaw, the third of K'ankin. [Illegible glyphs] will oc-cur. [Illegible glyphs] the descent of Bolon Yokte Ku (the Nine Foot Tree God) to [illegible glyphs]."[24]

Appearing a flimsy basis from which to draw apocalyptic conclusions, the insights offered by Monument 6 are sometimes bolstered by the *Chilam Balam*, volumes of folklore written by several shamans between the sixteenth and eighteenth centu-ries. Penned after the arrival of the Spanish and the Christian-ization of the culture—the *Chilam Balam* does not even mention the Long Count calendar, which had been abandoned more than a thousand years before. One entry, however, mentions a date

*Fig. 15_* ERODED AND CRACKED, MONUMENT 6 IN
TORTUGUERO, MEXICO, IS THE BASIS FOR THE
SO-CALLED MAYA PROPHECY

from the sacred fifty-two-year calendar—Four Ahaw. On that date, "The quetzal comes, the green bird comes. He of the yellow tree comes. Blood-vomit comes. K'uk'ulkan (an ancient god believed to Quatzalcoatl) shall come."[25] However, it's unclear exactly what year Four Ahaw is or whether it is noting a date in the past or future. It might be referring to 937 C.E., 1500 C.E., or perhaps 2012. Whatever this almanac is saying, it is not a message written by the ancient Maya, since it was penned long after their civilization had disappeared.

Modern Maya elders sometimes step up to the mike, but they give contradictory opinions about when the calendar ends and contradictory views about the meaning of the Long Count's rollover. Few believe it marks an apocalypse, though some say it marks the dawn of a new age. Besides, while the modern Maya appear to be the most legitimate contemporary source on the ancients, they long ago lost their link with the Classic Maya civilization. Until recently, they ignored the old sites, often building houses over their ancestors' tombs. They haven't written hieroglyphics for nearly five hundred years, and they stopped using the Long Count calendar five hundred years before that. Modern shamans still make prophecies, and many believe, as did the ancients, that Maya magicians can adopt animal forms, but most modern Maya are Catholic, their ancestors forced to abandon their faith when the Spanish showed up.

THE MODERN MAYA

Take a trip to Guatemala and ask about 2012, and most people you meet (the majority of whom are not Maya) are likely to tell you they don't give it much credence. Talk to the Maya, however, and the conversation may change. There are more than five million Maya in Guatemala, the stomping ground of their dramatic ancestors. As a result of wars through the centuries, including the Caste Wars in Central America, the Maya have become the region's poorest and most discriminated against; The United Nations says tens of thousands have been killed in recent decades by governments practicing what amounts to genocide. The Maya speak dozens of languages—including two that were spoken by the ancients—and some still use the old calendars— albeit the tzolkin and calendar round, not the Long Count that is ticking down to 2012. Some Maya are still tapped at an early age to become shamans, and fortune-telling is still a way of life. And some Maya elders are "day keepers" who chart the calendars and are speaking out about 2012:

DON ALEJANDRO PEREZ OXLAJ: Wandering Wolf, his sacred name, is a thirteenth-generation Maya medicine man and president of the National Mayan Council of Elders of Guatemala. He likes publicity and has flown to various parts of the world, including India, to speak on 2012. He takes tour groups to sacred sites for fire ceremonies, sacred cave meditations, and readings. He says the 2012-ers have it all wrong: The end of the calendar isn't until March 2013. Along with most Maya elders, he's annoyed at those who've hijacked and distorted Maya history and are issuing bogus prophecies and designing new lunar calendars.

CARLOS BARRIOS Born into a Spanish family in Guatemala, historian and anthropologist Barrios is not Maya by ethnicity, although he grew up among the Maya and studied the Mayan calendars with Maya elders for years—ultimately becoming a Mayan ceremonial priest and spiritual guide. He says the Maya are ticked off: "People write about prophecy in the name of the Maya. They say that the world will end in December 2012. The Mayan elders are angry with this. The world will not end. It will be transformed. The indigenous have the calendars, and know how to accurately interpret it, not others." In 2002, using the tzolkin calendar and calendar round, Barrios predicted upcoming turmoil with banks on a global scale, saying many could crash; he said that if the United States entered war with Iraq prior to April 2003, it would be bad but manageable, and if war started between April and July 2003 it would be disastrous. (It started March 20, 2003). He foresees a nuclear showdown between India and Pakistan in the near future, albeit one that's short-lived.

HUNBATZ MEN A respected Maya elder and shaman, Hunbatz Men was apparently the original source of the idea that the Maya were proficient space travelers and had mapped seven galaxies before coming here, an idea he passed on to José Argüelles. He is also a proponent of the idea that thirteen crystal skulls were created by the Maya and must be reunited before the world can know peace.

Scholars aren't even sure whether the Classic Maya regarded the beginning or end of the Long Count as more important. Were they actually backdating the calendar to a significant astronomical event in 3114 B.C.E., or were they highlighting a galactic event a thousand years into the future? And given the fact that they were intrigued by astrology and keen on prophecies—and could foresee events such as eclipses thousands of years in the future—why didn't they at least venture a guess about what the end date would signify? Or were they, like us,

*Fig.16_* HARMONIC CONVERGENCE *Famous for tooting on his wooden recorder in between rambling about the Maya, global rainbows, and galactic vibrations, José Argüelles (shown here playing on Mt. Shasta) is the pied piper of 2012. A major player in the New Age movement and organizer of the 1987 Harmonic Convergence, the former art history professor who claims he can channel Maya god-king Lord Pakal has authored esoteric books, developed a galactically attuned calendar, and hyped the ending of the Maya Long Count calendar as portending a reality shattering moment. His fans are many; his foes include Maya elders who disagree with his interpretations and fear he's falsely representing himself and Maya culture.*

simply more concerned with their present than about a date a thousand years in the future, as David Stuart argues. The answer simply isn't clear.

So if the ancient Maya didn't write it, then where did this idea of a Maya prophecy come from? Why do even esteemed futurologists embed this idea of the "famous Mayan prophecy" that will bring "an end of this world as we know it" into their writings? What has triggered a tidal wave of half-truths, galactic babblings, fear, and hopeful preparations for a new day?

The answer appears to be José Argüelles, PhD, a thin, gray-haired, long-faced flutist and art historian now in his seventies, who by his own admission is a probable alien/galactic agent. Said to be telepathic, he also claims to be a channeler. He is definitely the author of impenetrably abstract books. The way José Argüelles, PhD, put the 2012 phenomenon in motion: the Harmonic Convergence.

The two-day event he organized in August 1987 theoretically drew from a prophecy by Quetzalcoatl: José Argüelles, PhD, warned that just about anything could happen over those days—including catastrophic events—unless 144,000 people joined in and put out harmonious emotions; then the Harmonic Convergence could herald a new era of peace, joy, illumination, and solar power—simply through humming and meditation. The crystallization point for the New Age movement, the hum-in served as a great publicity tool. It also stamped the date December 21, 2012, into the minds of the New Age masses—and the idea that the date would mark the end of the world as we know it. Among the promised highlights of 2012: humans and aliens will finally meet up. Never mind that Argüelles said the same thing would happen back in 1992.

THE HARMONIC CONVERGENCE

When he met Tony Shearer and learned about Quetzalcoatl's supposed prophecy, José Argüelles ran with the idea. He created the 1987 event that would be known as the Harmonic Convergence as a José Argüelles, PhD, production, complete with press releases, pronouncements about the future of the world, explanations about the Long Count calendar, and a book, *The Mayan Factor*, which introduced "José Argüelles logic" and even handy "José Argüelles formulas," such as "Myth = DNA x Light"—the meaning of which is as mystifying and vague as the entire contents of the book.

Those who found themselves boggled by his obtuse writing could find analysis of the book's meaning—and the meaning of the Harmonic Convergence itself—in the flood of interviews of and articles by Argüelles popping up everywhere from the *New York Times* to the *Washington Post*. He told the *Wall Street Journal* that he'd come up with the date that marked "the point at which the counter-spin of history finally comes to a momentary halt, and the still imperceptible spin of post-history commences," while meditating atop a Mayan pyramid. Fortuitously, the stars, it was announced, would form a rare alignment between sun, moon, Venus, and Mars on August 16 and 17. He called for 144,000 souls—a number that he'd reportedly pulled from the Bible's book of Revelation as well as the Mayan calendar—to gather on sacred spots and harmonize the Earth's energy. Apparently our planet's "vibratory infrastructure" was experiencing a bad case of "resonant dissonance" thanks to wars, arms races, and fossil fuels, and it needed to be grounded.[26]

Even though Shearer had been writing about an Aztec god, Quetzalcoatl, when he met with Argüelles, the event spun by Argüelles was linked definitively to the Maya, who were suddenly being repackaged. Argüelles planted ideas about ancient prophecies and extraterrestrial origins all over the place. "At 5:55 A.M. next Sunday, according to an ancient Mayan prophecy, a new age of peace and harmony will dawn," reported the *Chicago Sun-Times* in the days leading up to the Harmonic Convergence, running with a prophecy that the Maya had never made and adding without a hint of irony that the Mayan calendars had been created by aliens from the Galactic Federation.[27] Argüelles explained on a public radio station in Colorado that Earth had been passing through a "Galactic Synchronization Beam" that had been ionizing us evolutionarily for thousands of years. "According to the Mayan calendar, we're a little more than twenty-five years away from departing from the beam we've been in since 3113 B.C.," he said, managing not only to get the calendar start date wrong (it's 3114 B.C.E.), but to link it to a beam that apparently only he knew about, since scientists are as clueless about it as the Maya, modern or ancient. The Classic Maya, he informed eager reporters, were "galactic surfers." They had mapped out seven galaxies, he'd recently learned; the Mayan calendar code was a galactic code, the master code of the universe, the program for DNA, the I Ching, even the Bible's book of Revelation—or "book of Revelations," as he always referred to it, incorrectly.

His Harmonic Convergence, even if well intentioned, made some roll their eyes—*Doonesbury* cartoonist Garry Trudeau called it "The Moronic Convergence," and astrologers noted that there wasn't a grand trine in the planetary alignment for those days. But what bothered Maya scholars was Argüelles's casual approach toward facts, not the least of which was asserting that the original Maya were extraterrestrials. But, even if the stars didn't line up, even if scholars scoffed—and called him "a nutcase" in the *New York Times*—believers showed up all from over the world, far more than the 144,000 envisioned, reported Global Family, the public relations firm organizing the event. Thousands showed up at the great pyramid in Giza, ambled up Mt. Shasta in California, meditated on Indian mounds in the American Midwest, and chanted at Hawaiian volcanoes, Mayan pyramids, and Aztec temples. Tens of thousands of well-wishers gathering to save the world by doing what Argüelles had instructed them to do: hum, hold hands, and send out peaceful vibes as they prepared for that moment twenty-five years away when the calendar would end, and so would the world as we know it.

Despite substantial chortling about the matter, the Iran-Iraq War ended the next year, the Berlin Wall soon crumbled, the Soviet Union fell apart—all happenings which at least some of those in attendance credited the Harmonic Convergence with creating. They're not copping to the hum-in's effects (or lack thereof) on Desert Storm, the rise of al-Qaeda, and the emergence of the Taliban in Afghanistan; apparently humming can only work its magic so far.

Reportedly honored at a meeting of Mayan elders a few years back, Argüelles took the mantle of being "the closer of the cycle"—supervising the end of this baktun, a title that Mayan elders have since unsuccessfully asked him to drop. Before long he had immersed himself in the role of self-appointed Maya messenger, issuing prophecies and commands about how life needed to change in order to ensure human survival. After writing a book about galactic surfing across outer space and through Earth with a Maya spirit, he and his wife, Lloydine, assumed the titles "galactic peace missionaries"—roles that he claims they were "commanded" to take by Maya spirits.

Their mission: to change time. All of the world's problems, says Argüelles, stem from the Gregorian calendar—"the world's most insidious dogma," "a tool of the Vatican" that the Catholic Church uses to "maintain mind control over the human species,"[28] with its emphasis on twelve months, irregularly numbered, and filled with sixty-minute hours. However, all of the world's many woes could be solved, says Argüelles, by the adoption of his new Dreamspell—a thirteen-moon, twenty-eight-day calendar of months with names like Yellow Cosmic Seed in years called things such as Blue Electric Storm.

The Dreamspell calendar isn't the Maya calendar, but it is interwoven with the Mayan code and Mayan mathematics. What's more, it embraces "the law of time" that has been revealed to Argüelles by no less than Lord Pakal, whom he claims to channel. And the law of time, specifically "Energy factored by Time equals Art," "accounts for the intrinsic elegance of all natural phenomena," says the site for the Galactic Research Institution of the Foundation for the Law of Time, an outfit he set up and directs. The Law of Time even explains psychic phenomena: "The corollary formulation of the Law of Time states that the velocity of time is instantaneously infinite, a factor which accounts for telepathy and various paranormal phenomena."[29]

But the most important concept of the Law of Time is that humans cease defining time in the "aberration of artificial time" that is measured with segments of 12:60—as in twelve months and measures of sixty minutes and sixty seconds—and reattune themselves to the vibration of 13:20, as in thirteen moons and twenty twenty-eight-day months, a rhythm that reflects the changing vibrations of our planet, claims Argüelles.

Argüelles's calendar-changing mission—to substitute his "cosmically harmonic" calendar for the deviant calendar currently in use—is so urgent that he has written to both the pope and the United Nations, formally demanding a timekeeping change to rescue the planet. Only adoption of his "13 Moon" calendar, he insists, can bring world peace. "Because it is a perfect harmonic standard, peace is inherent in the thirteen Moon twenty-eight-day synchronometer [calendar]," he explains. "This frequency shift itself establishes a new foundation for everyday life where harmony is peace and time is art."[30]

Beyond promoting his new Dreamspell calendar and spouting about his related Law of Time, a law as significant as the law of gravity, he says, Argüelles has begun issuing prophecies from Lord Pakal (whom he refers to as Galactic Agent 13 66 56). Initially "channeling" Pakal, José Argüelles revealed that he was also an incarnation of the royal, as well as his messenger, Valum Votan. "Through my knowledge and life-time work," he announced, "I am the heir of the legacy of [Lord] Pacal Votan and the instrument of his prophecy, Telektonon."[31]

The modern Maya began disassociating from Argüelles, claiming he's hijacked the Mayan calendar, which he's distorted and changed. They were in an uproar about his claim of being the messenger and incarnation of Lord Pakal. The elders demanded he drop the name and step out of their game. Scholars were in an uproar as well: Little that Argüelles said had any basis in fact—he was spewing misinformation across the Internet, in interviews, in books, and on YouTube. But by then, 2012 had taken on a life of its own. Argüelles countered that he was the legitimate Maya messenger here to end the great cycle and asserted that without him there would be no 2012, no Mayan resurgence, no interest in the calendar—and in that last case at least he may have been right.

While Argüelles—oops, make that Valum Votan, since he announced that José Argüelles, PhD, was dead—continued spouting about the common end date when humans had to conquer the world of machines by envisioning rainbows around the planet, others jumped in with ideas that ranged from interesting to slightly plausible to absurd, leaving those following the trend to pick and choose which they believed.

A VARIETY PACK OF 2012-ERS

The voices crying out in the 2012 cacophony are diverse, but they can be generally broken into a few groups:

MODERN SHAMANS Hallucinogens, drug-induced trances, and visions are the hallmark of this bunch, who tend to see the world via their navel and often overlap cultural references, weaving the wisdom of the I Ching in with astrology and the Mayan calendar, for instance. Under this umbrella, one finds Terence McKenna, Daniel Pinchbeck, and, of course, José Argüelles.

SCHOLARLY ENTHUSIASTS Prone to intuitive leaps but writing in more rigorous manners than the modern shamans, this group puts forward specific theories and engages in debates as heated as those of nineteenth-century scholars. John Major Jenkins, Carl Johan Calleman, and Ray Mardyks top the list—and their feuds are legendary.

IMAGINARY SCIENTISTS They pull from science but amplify it with fear, resulting in ideas that may be illuminating but come off as being close to hysterical. Gregg Braden, who warns of a possible polar reversal on Earth, and Lawrence E. Joseph, who warns about the same event (as well as devastating solar storms), fall into this group.

FUTURE THINKERS Futurologists and systems analysts have joined in—pointing to problems and needed transitions, but often not defining the steps needed to get there. Ervin László and Barbara Marx Hubbard top this list.

HYSTERICS Much of the information found on the Internet fits into this category. 2012 marks the end of the world according to the Maya, Aztec, Hopi, Jews, Hindus, Edgar Cayce, Nostradamus, St. Malachy, and/or Merlin according to this bunch, who assure us that the poles are reversing, Yellowstone is rumbling, and/or a Mars-size comet is whipping our way.

In recent years, the 2012 thinkers, writers, prophets, and promoters have collectively become a churning 2012 PR machine, thumping out wildly colorful ideas. A few of their sometimes contradictory assertions:

- The crop-circle enthusiasts point out that the designs of the circles are becoming more detailed and appear to be bringing in Mayan motifs, and some assert that the electromagnetic energy has changed in the ground under the designs.

- Some Maya day keepers say that 2012 will spur a spiritual leap, but the dates aren't hammered down: Some say the calendar actually doesn't end until 2013.

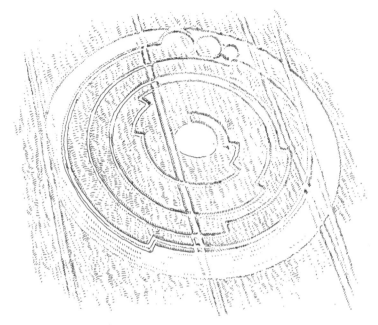

*Fig. 17_*WHATEVER IS CREATING CROP CIRCLES, THOSE
WHO FOLLOW THEM SAY THEY ARE GROWING MORE
DETAILED IN DESIGN.

- Swedish author Carl Johan Calleman said that, based on his calculations about the Maya's Nine Underworlds, the Long Count calendar will actually turn its final day in 2011; he later revised his calculations, marking the final day as occurring in the summer of 2012.

- Since 1914, the Hopi have discussed their prophecies about the appearance of the Blue Star—a vague notion that some believe may be a comet, others a falling space lab—as a sign of doom.

▶ Nostradamus was apparently a little off with his prediction that the world would end in 1999. Back in his day they were using the Julian calendar, which must have marred his calculations.

▶ The end date of an ancient Indian calendar, Huta Gula, has been altered by some swamis and gurus and is now reckoned (by some) to end in 2012, and there were more coincidences: The Hindi word *maya* means "magic of the gods" and "world of illusion," which also seems to tie in.

▶ The constellation the Pleiades—the Seven Sisters—is studied for more meaning because the first star is named Maya, and the Maya had studied the constellation as well.

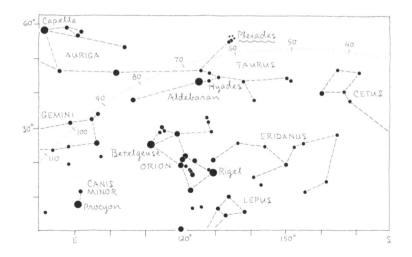

*Fig.18_* MAYA STARGAZERS WERE FASCINATED BY THE PLEIADES

- Buddha was snared in the debate: He'd never predicted anything about 2012 or an End Times, but his mom's name was Maya, it was said.

- Star watcher Ray Mardyks began toying with the idea that the Long Count calendar was related to the nearly 26,000-year-long precession of the equinoxes, during which the position of our North Star appears to shift and then returns to its original placement in the sky. The calendar, after all, marked just about one-fifth of the time—and the Maya believed that the length of five Long Count calendars marked one Great Age.

- John Major Jenkins took Mardyks's ideas further and asserted that, during the solstice of December 21, 2012, the Sun will be aligned with the center of the Milky Way. He made this theory the foundation of his book *Maya Cosmogenesis 2012*. He supported the idea with art, architecture, and alignment of ball courts and temples of an Olmec/Mayan site in Izapa. The Maya, he said, were clearly trying to point out this alignment, signaling a time of massive change.

- Believers in planet Nibiru, a hurtling orb which some fear is on a collision course with Earth, joined in. The "existence" of this apparently mythological planet was brought to light by the writings of Israeli journalist Zecharia Sitchin, who derived his ideas from the Bible and archeological studies in Iraq. He says Nibiru's inhabitants, the Anunnaki, brought information to ancient Sumer and warned that Nibiru would ultimately demolish the Earth. The exact details, however, were apparently lost—he says because the Anunnaki inadvertently destroyed the Sumerian civilization in 2024 B.C.E. when Nibiru's warring clans used "nuclear weapons to obliterate their spaceport in the Sinai Peninsula." Sitchin himself has kept mum on the precise dates when Nibiru is supposed to smack us. Some of those swept away by his ideas warned that Nibiru would slam into Earth in 2003; they've since changed the date to 2012.

➤ Science writers, pseudoscience writers, and astrologers join in talking about the possibility of a magnetic pole reversal, solar flares destroying our satellite system, and Yellowstone blowing its stack and blowing away our atmosphere.

➤ Tripping writer Terence McKenna predicted that everything that could change would change by 2012.

➤ Futurologists threaded 2012 fantasies into their projections and facts, speaking of ancient Mayan prophecies that fore-told of a needed leap.

➤ Writer Daniel Pinchbeck—like McKenna, one of our self-appointed modern shamans—fell under the 2012 spell and began taking a cocktail of trip inducers to figure out what it all meant, interviewing everyone from José Argüelles, PhD, to praying mantises—who informed him they were galactic emissaries—as part of his research.

➤ Christian "endtimers" embraced the furor created by the Maya calendar as just another indication of upcoming termi-nation. The late Jerry Falwell, among others, predicted the end was near, and since it didn't happen during 2000, regarded by Falwell and others as a likely moment for the apocalypse,[32] the upcoming apocalypse was hooked, by some, onto the tale of the rising 2012 star. Argüelles had even welcomed evangelicals into his club, saying in his fifty-seventh prophecy of Lord Pakal that "One special voice did this Jesus have, a man named Saint John of Patmos, in whom the gift of prophecy was fulfilled." Saint John, of course, is most famous for Revelation, the last book of the New Testament, often cited by the crowd that follows the End Times.

The 2004 tsunami, Hurricane Katrina, a crashing economy, and ongoing wars—disturbing enough by themselves—seemed more proof of the end when viewed through the 2012 prism. Survivalists began stocking up and boning up on their back-to-earth basics, sales of bomb shelters soared, 2012 survival guides began hitting the bookstands, doomsday clocks began ticking down, and Internet site after Internet site talked of the ancient Maya prophecy that had foretold of this era of gloom. José Argüelles, PhD, began instructing his followers to think even more positively—that together they could have the effect of a positive nuclear bomb—and forestall the calamities ahead. And then Sony released *2012*—a movie about the end of the world by tidal wave, earthquake, and every other means of destruction—and created their faux professional organization, the Institute for Human Continuity (http://www.institutefor humancontinuity.org), to stir up the angst.

Given the high-pitched conjecturing and far-fetched ideas that have previously accompanied study of the Maya, what has happened with 2012 should be absolutely no surprise—which is to say, facts regarding it have been shaped and twisted. It shouldn't come as a shock that the buzz about the winter solstice on 12/21/12 has amplified to near-deafening levels around the world, eliciting dire warnings alongside promises of the chance for a new-and-improved global society.

Passionate theories, extreme interpretations, and fantasy-filled dreaminess are apparently par for the course any time you're dealing with the Maya.

A SHORT ROUND UP

So, with all the shouting that's going on, what exactly does 2012 mean? Here is a short round-up by some of the best-known voices.

CARL JOHAN CALLEMAN "At the present time we are beginning to enter the eighth level of consciousness of the cosmic pyramid, based on the foundation provided by the seven lower levels. This eighth level may be referred to as the galactic frame of conscious-ness as it will step by step lead humanity to identify primarily with the galaxy. The highest level of consciousness, the Universal, will be attained through the workings of the Ninth Underworld in the year 2011 and will result in a timeless cosmic consciousness, and a citizen-ship in the universe, on the part of humanity."[33]

TERENCE MCKENNA "[T]he end-date for my own mushroom-revealed model of the cosmos ended on the same date as the Maya calendar . . . the world is to be born at last on December 21, 2012 A.D."[34]

JOHN MAJOR JENKINS "On 13.0.0.0.0 in the Long Count Calendar— what we would call December 21, 2012—the Maya expected nothing short of the rebirth of the world . . . The 2012 era is about the birth of something new on this planet, but it is also a death, the rupture of the womb-world . . . the 2012 era represents a global reversal."[35]

ASSORTED NEW AGE SITES "7th century Mayan prophet Pacal Votan left a universal message . . . alerting present-day humanity that our biological process is transforming, approaching the culmination of a 26,000 year evolutionary program [that] will culminate on the winter solstice, December 21, 2012 A.D. . . . This time we are now in has been called "The Time of Trial on Earth," "Judgement Day," "The Time of Great Purification," "The End of this Creation," "The Quickening," "The End of Time as We Know It," [and] "The Shift of the Ages."[36]

JOSÉ ARGÜELLES "The meaning of 2012 lies in our waking up to the actual nature of time . . . Earth is not a spaceship but a timeship, and . . . the purpose of operating in the 13:20 frequency of galactic time is to transform the planet into a work of art."

PROFESSOR DAVID STUART The rollover date of Long Count calendar marks "a special anniversary of creation. The Maya never said the world is going to end, they never said anything bad would happen necessarily, they're just recording this future anniversary on Monument 6." [37]

Whatever one thinks about 2012 and the varied "cult of ideas" that surrounds it, the event is yet another illustration of the enduring hold of this remarkable civilization. The Maya, a people virtually unknown to the world until two hundred years ago, now exert more power worldwide than they did at the pinnacle of their civilization. They've inadvertently played roles in wars; they've been indirectly responsible for the rebirth of ideas like the lost continent of Atlantis. And now, even though they didn't say much about it, if anything at all, their calendar is the source of a dark fear that hangs overhead. Like few before them, the Maya, their ideas, and ideas conceived upon discovery of them continue to haunt the thinking of humankind, even if humans aren't aware that the Maya, or discovery of their vanished world, is the source. A thousand years after the light flickered out on their golden era, the Maya are still catalysts and ionizers—changing not only the way we view their past but also the way we see our future. And their monuments and lost cities continue to awe, even as we continue to suffer from Maya madness.

The 2012 phenomenon itself—mostly a fabrication that has little to do with the Maya, being linked to the ideas of Argüelles, and furthered along to a new level of hooey by Sony Pictures—might be amusing, were it not scaring the heck out of people. And the reason it is resonating with some is that humanity does indeed have problems, big, big problems. But, like the 2012 phenomenon itself, most of them are human creations, and most are of recent origin. In chapter 4, we'll explore what science brings to the story—some of the reports more startling than the bogus info spread by 2012-ers.

Perhaps December 21, 2012, does indeed mark the end of the world or the beginning of a cataclysmic era, or even a portal that will allow humans to make a spiritual, evolutionary leap. However, there isn't one scrap of evidence that the ancient Maya said that, believed it, or were the source of that belief. In fact, perhaps Hollywood and the History Channel are barking up the wrong tree: the Mayan Long Count calendar was not even devised by the Maya, being in fact a product of a different Mesoamerican civilization—the Olmec, whose world disappeared with little trace centuries before the Maya's. Apparently, the ancient Olmec aren't available to be wheeled out for comment.

SCIENCE
WEIGHS IN
Sifting Through Facts and Fantasies

Perhaps the idea of an apocalyptic or era-changing event in 2012 rings true for many, particularly Americans, simply because as a species we are in need of a shake-up. Our war-dependent, resource-depleting global civilization does not appear sustainable for many centuries, even decades, into the future. We are already in a transition energy-wise, as we search for new sources to power our cars and heat our homes. Across the planet, we've been witnessing political realignments, with the downfall of the Soviet Union, the rise of the European Union, and new alliances across Asia and South America. Technology is boosting our world into novel realms, for better or worse—with everything from lasers and drones to global positioning systems and the

Internet—although the question looming before us is how much we will rule our machines and how much they will rule us. Technologically, politically, environmentally, even economically, our world does appear to be at a crossroads—some might say it hovers at the brink.

Up to this point, 2012 may sound like trippy nonsense spewed by navel gazers, fanatics, and gloomsters. The scenario presented by New Dawners is a dazzling mix of multicultural myth, theater, and "prophecy," but their position is likewise characterized by alarming inattention to accuracy. Those tending to the facts—scholars, archeologists, astronomers, and scientists—get the cold shoulder from mystical sorts—scientists and statisticians aren't invited to speak at the New Dawners' 2012 conventions, their touch of reality unwelcome.

The frosty feeling is mutual: Most scientists scoff at an end of the world foretold by prophets, planetary alignments, and ancient calendars. Academics are openmouthed at what's spouting off the lips of many 2012-ers, whom they dismiss as dramatic storytellers. And the showdown is fiercest at NASA, where writers of columns such as "Ask an Astrophysicist" are bristling at the thousands of letters asking about an incoming attack by Planet X and Nibiru, and if Earth will be sucked into the Milky Way's black hole on the ill-fated winter solstice.

But this is where the 2012 story twists. While the pictures painted on the Internet and scribbled in books often fall somewhere between exaggeration and hooey, when science strolls into the scenario, 2012 changes entirely and becomes a far more serious matter. Scientists, including biologists, physicists, and social scientists such as demographers and sociologists, keep showing us proof that our world is crashing into a wall. Or, rather,

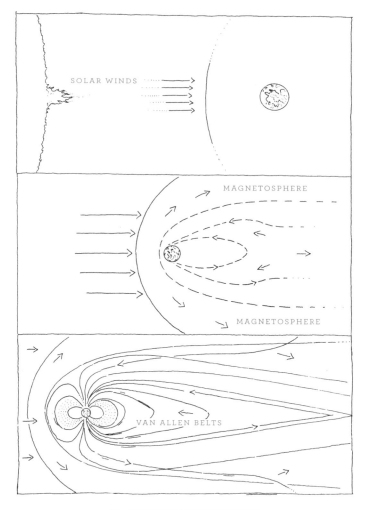

*Fig.19_*THE MAGNETOSPHERE

Top: Solar winds move toward the earth.
Middle: Earth's Magnetosphere deflects solar winds and plasma.
Bottom: The Van Allen Belts, altered by nuclear tests in
the 1960s, still work.

scientists are pointing out that we're driving our world smack-dab into it—and the activities of the world's militaries aren't helping. Unlike the future spun by 2012 dream weavers, who portray us as victims—whether of Maya time-telling circumstance, galactic churning, or political spinning—scientists often underscore our active involvement in the state of the planet.

Science—the agreed-upon version of the reality of our existence based on our measurements, experiments, and study of cycles—gives the most compelling evidence that the thirteenth baktun is turning over in a most precarious time and that something is indeed going awry on our lovely planet. Not the least of our problems is a thinning and ripped-up magnetic "shield," or magnetosphere, some 400 miles above us.

Reports of what's happening in the "heavens," where the Maya were prone to gaze, are just one place where scientific warnings grow eerie, inadvertently supporting assorted 2012 scenarios. Get ready for blackouts and the sound of silence: Our electrical grids and telecommunication systems may be fried by incoming solar flares and electromagnetic storms. The National Research council of the National Academies is warning of a potential "Space Storm Katrina"—extreme space weather fueled by the magnetic activity of the sun. Everything from aircraft communication to pipeline operation may be at risk, according to the council's 2008 publication, *Severe Space Weather Events*. And such a Space Katrina could unfold in the very near future.

"[W]e're in for a tough time in the next eleven years," David Sibeck of NASA's Goddard Space Flight Center in Maryland told geophysicists last year, predicting some of history's most violent geomagnetic storms and biggest disturbances of the radiation belts surrounding the Earth.[38] The reason: a little snag in the electrically charged "bubble"—the magnetosphere or Van Allen belt—that deflects solar flares from Earth. It's been weakening for decades, but in late 2008 NASA discovered that it's ripping—a problem that could produce all kinds of costly migraines, from messing up satellites to zapped electrical power grids. And when are these problems most likely to kick up? During the expected "solar maximum"—when sunspots, flares, and solar winds peak—in 2012.

Astrophysicists warn that, starting in 2012, magnetic storms may be their most intense since 1958, a year of very peculiar weather, when electromagnetic energy swirled in our atmosphere in ways it never had before—a year from which some say our atmosphere never has fully recovered. That year at least, you couldn't point at Mother Nature as the culprit for the odd weather. That year the fluke storms and strange sunsets had everything to do with the U.S. Department of Defense.

SECRET SPACE WARS

The Maya didn't know about the magnetosphere—or, if they did, they didn't mention it. Modern science didn't even discover this "layer" that swirls between 400 and 40,000 miles above the planet until February 1958, after *Explorer I*, the first U.S. satellite, was launched. This gaseous, electromagnetic, cylindrical "shell" shields Earth from harmful solar energy and 500-mile-per-hour winds and has been a source of fascination ever since its discovery.

NASA says their recent unexpected find—of a breach in the shell four times larger than Earth—isn't caused by human activities.[39]

Despite their assurances, there is certainly reason to wonder: The last time we had extremely violent solar storms, in 1958, they were right on the heels of nuclear bomb tests in the upper atmosphere. During the Cold War, the militaries of the United States and the Soviet Union conducted a number of secret experiments—now openly admitted to by the Defense Nuclear Agency—that were staggeringly dangerous given the magnetosphere's crucial role in protecting our planet.[40] The U.S. Department of Defense initially planned to war-proof the upper parts of the stratosphere, thinking that the natural version should be replaced with a human-made model that would allow U.S. military radio and radar to function after a nuclear war—certainly a legitimate concern, but one that might not warrant rearranging the stratosphere.

Doing preliminary research for that new-and-improved upper atmosphere plan, the U.S. Department of Defense began exploding nuclear and hydrogen devices hundreds of miles overhead. According to a 1996 article written by physicist Rosalie Bertell for *Earthpulse Press* and subsequently reprinted on the site of the Global Policy Forum think tank, in the summer of 1958 the U.S. Navy blasted three nuclear bombs and two hydrogen bombs some 400 miles above Earth—wreaking havoc and creating an artificial radiation belt that wrapped around the planet, admittedly making for some gorgeous auroras.[41] Again, in 1962, after the Soviets dropped a test-ban treaty, the U.S. military began nuclear tests in the stratosphere—essentially destroying the Van Allen radiation belt overhead for months and altering its shape and density for centuries to come. The matter was little helped when the overhead nuclear bomb-a-thon was matched by the Soviets, who created three additional belts of radiation around the Earth. [42]

The 1962 incident was such a fiasco that plans for future nuclear tests in the upper levels of the stratosphere were quickly dropped, but military activities have continued to wear on the stratosphere.[43] When one considers the dozens of nuclear weapons tests, the reported but still hushed use of electromagnetic pulse weapons by the U.S. in Desert Storm, and the release of radioactive gases from nuclear facilities, the appearance of holes in the magnetosphere might not seem so natural after all.

Whether caused by long-ago nuclear tests, ongoing climate change, the cyclic reversal of the sun's poles, or the planet's military-supervised "ionospheric heaters"—which zap radio waves into the ionosphere just to see what will happen—the damage to the magnetosphere is only one change charging the atmosphere with fear.

The slow migration of the magnetic poles is well documented— the North Pole has been shifting toward Siberia—but lately the level of the Earth's magnetism has been dropping so much that some people speculate that a polar reversal could be underway. Proponents of 2012 theories have portrayed this as an event that takes place overnight, while scientists downplay the idea of a sudden reversal, and say that such a reversal, should it occur, is probably thousands of years away. And unlike forecasts given on plenty of "2012: the end" sites on the Internet, such a pole reversal—should it take place—doesn't appear to have anything to do with our position in the Milky Way.

Yet there are galactic phenomena that are raising the eyebrows of scientists. Mirroring concerns of some 2012-ers, some scientists are beginning to grow antsy that we could be knocked permanently out of commission by a planet-buster from the sky. They are not talking about Planet X or Nibiru, however, both of which appear to be mythical creations. They are instead looking at the millions upon millions of pieces of rock and dirty ice that venture near the Earth as they orbit. The danger for us is that one of these comets, asteroids, or other "near-Earth objects" gets pulled close enough to Earth's gravitational field to become, essentially, a high-speed Earth-bound "bomb."

Small asteroids, a few inches or feet wide, land here frequently—making contact with our planet typically near the poles or in the deserts of the Middle East. But some asteroids are huge, ten miles in diameter or more, and when they slam into Earth—their speeds increasing as they come into our atmosphere—the ramifications are huge.

"It's not a matter of if, but when we get smacked by a planet buster," says longtime space watcher Theresa Hitchens,[44] not speaking in her official capacity as director of the United Nations Institute for Disarmament Research. After all, a hurtling asteroid, a whopping 11 miles in diameter, brought mass extinction 65 million years ago when it dropped into our world: Oddly enough, it fell in the heart of what would become Maya land, the Yucatán peninsula.

ASTEROIDAL AND COMETARY CONSIDERATIONS

Ignatius Donnelly was the porcine-faced, nineteenth-century congressman and utopian who, in his best-selling 1882 book *Atlantis, the Antediluvian World*, stamped the idea of the lost continent into the public mind (and also the idea that the original Maya had escaped from there) and inadvertently helped to fuel the rise of Hitler (see page 78). He also wheeled out two other

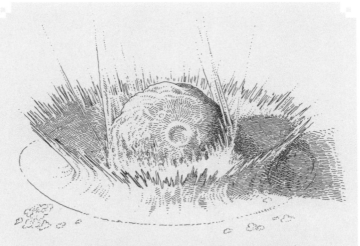

***Fig.20*_CATASTROPHE-CREATING COMET CHICXULUB**

popular notions for which he is likewise forgotten as the source. He was apparently the first to propose in a book that playwright William Shakespeare was actually Sir Francis Bacon—starting a debate that continues in thespian and literary circles. He also got readers of the 1880s fired up about comets. He suggested that a high-speed comet had smacked into our planet unleashing global chaos from earthquakes to an ice age long ago. What's more, he suggested that a comet would be back for a repeat performance, using assorted Indian legends, including those of the Chickasaws and Pueblo as well as the post-Columbian Maya, to support the idea. In *Ragnarok: The Age of Fire and Gravel*, he wrote that, "The Mayas of Yucatán had a prediction which Father Lizana, curé of Itzamal, preserved in the Spanish language:

> *'At the close of the ages, it hath been decreed,*
> *Shall perish and vanish each weak god of men,*
> *And the world shall be purged with ravening fire.'"*[45]

Although he delighted the literate masses, he was laughed off by the scientific community for his colliding comet theory, as well as for the idea that there would be an encore.

A century later, however, Donnelly was vindicated—as were several late-twentieth-century scientists who had postulated the same, with more details on the mass extinction and ice age that followed. In the 1970s, an oil prospector came across something unusual just to the north of the Yucatán peninsula near the city of Chicxulub: a crater more than 100 miles wide. It wasn't until the 1990s that the story was put together of a fiery asteroid five times wider than Manhattan that had crashed into Earth with a tremendous impact—millions of times stronger than the most powerful bomb yet known—a crash that unleashed global shock waves, devastating earthquakes, megatsunamis, planetwide volcanoes, and endless fires that spewed nonstop even through torrential storms of acid rain. So much ash, smoke, and dust was put into the atmosphere that the greenhouse effect came into the play. We all now know what happened next. The Earth was sealed off from the sun. Glaciers and ice masses covered the land. Dinosaurs soon perished; cut off from sunlight, plankton died with disastrous chain reactions that wiped out any remaining life in the seas; and plants on terra firma withered away. As a result of the oversized, high-speed rock, more than three-quarters of life on the planet disappeared.

While he was off in his terminology—what blasted the planet was an asteroid, not a comet, which is made of dirty ice—Donnelly, more a dreamer than a scientist, was right. Now, some scientists even believe that a collision with a celestial object the size of Mars created our moon. Donnelly's related idea—that a large comet would show up again with apocalyptic results—has mostly been a feature in End Times hysteria and sci-fi novels; the effects of a "planet buster" weren't seriously contemplated by scientists until recently.

A few years ago, however, astronomers caught sight of a new asteroid—called 99942 Apophis—that looked like it might smack us hard on April 13, 2029; it also swings by in 2013 and 2021. NASA dismisses it as a close call—the odds are now about 3 percent that it will hit Earth, but the asteroid's proximity has generated a new wave of thought: We'd better get ready. Astronaut Rusty Schweickart is so alarmed and convinced of the dangers that he put together the B612 Foundation to formulate plans and lobby the government to prepare for taking down incoming near-Earth objects (NEOs).

Given the vast array of weapons at our disposal, one might think that comet target practice would be a breeze, but it's not. Schweickart says we currently don't have the technology or know-how to tackle an NEO, particularly one 10 miles wide or greater. Statistically speaking, these asteroids become dangerously attracted to Earth every 10 million years.

The Chicxulub asteroid, in fact, actually proved more important to the Maya than their revered timekeeping methods: The massive chunk of rock and its resulting crater, which became an acidic lake, ultimately created a series of sinkholes and a snaking limestone water network throughout the Yucatán peninsula. Millions of years later, those sinkholes and the subterranean hydrological network would provide the water necessary to sustain Mayan society. Maya farmers tapped them for irrigation, and the sinkholes themselves became sacred ceremonial sites seen as portals to the underworld.

The Chicxulub asteroid is a tale for us as well, one pertinent to 2012. It gives us a warning and a now-clear picture of how climate change can quickly wreak havoc and suck life out of

Earth. This historical scenario of our planet in shock—a reaction to the asteroid's thunderous arrival—isn't well known; besides, warnings about a near future when oceans spill over coastlines and fertile fields turn into sun-blasted deserts haven't spurred all that much action. And so history is repeating.

Our climate is changing, some parts warming, some parts cooling. Ice on the arctic sea shelf is 39 percent thinner than it was in 1979, and sea levels have risen by 50 millimeters since 1992. Some warn that sea levels could soon rise by several feet, meaning we'd be kissing places like Holland, the Maldives, and Japan goodbye, along with the cities on both American coasts. Drought is spreading like a terra virus. We're apparently beginning to see the effects of accumulated greenhouse gases—at least that's what's typically pointed to as the cause of recent bouts of strange and frightening weather—from tsunamis to flash floods and earthquakes. More than any other factor, those severe weather changes can trigger panic that doom-and-gloomers are right, the end is near.

Human activities—as well as those of our corporations and governments—are seriously pushing it, testing the limits. Every American schoolchild has been taught that deforestation, cars, factories, and power plants are creating climate-changing greenhouse gases, but the effects of military tests on our weather are less publicized. That 10-million-square-mile hole in the ozone layer that filters out ultraviolet waves was blamed on our lifestyle—aerosol sprays and chlorofluorocarbons in air conditioners and refrigerators were pointed to as the cause. However, far worse offenders are rockets. The 1975 launch of the *Saturn V* rocket literally burned a hole in the ionosphere, and every rocket that goes up—over five hundred a year—releases a ton of ozone-disintegrating gases.

And perhaps there's likewise more to the changing climate story than we're being told. Several governments apparently now possess the ability to alter weather—China recently announced it had created a snowstorm over Tibet. And it appears that the United States and probably Russia as well possess the technology to play God with the weather. If one is to believe William Cohen, secretary of defense under president Bill Clinton, terrorist groups may also have the capability. In April 1997, William Cohen remarked at a conference at the University of Georgia that some terrorists "are engaging even in an eco-type of terrorism whereby they can alter the climate, set off earthquakes, volcanoes remotely through the use of electromagnetic waves." [46]

Cynics might conclude that if terrorists hold that capability, governments with cutting-edge militaries do too. Controlling weather as a potential weapon has been a stated U.S. military goal for decades. This means that some of the strange weather we've been seeing may be more than acts of gods. Perhaps we are seeing a new kind of war—or at least the results of tests for a new kind of war.

"War is no longer about blowing holes in people," says Dr. Nick Begich, an author in Anchorage, Alaska, who's spent over 2 million dollars of his own money to publicize what is going on in nearby Gakona. "What is happening here marks a huge jump: we're looking at the ability to manipulate the whole environment as a weapon." [47]

What he's talking about: an experimental research center in southeastern Alaska. A field of dozens of oversized antennae, the High Frequency Active Auroral Research Program (HAARP) is the world's biggest radio transmitter. What gets some folks up there worried—even the legislature of the

European Union and Russia are up in arms and have issued calls for a moratorium on this military-funded project that beams focused rays of light into the ionosphere and magneto-sphere—is evidence that those experiments, well, they just might have everything to do with manipulating weather. The Defense Advanced Research Projects Agency (DARPA), the U.S. military's special research unit that runs the project, denies that HAARP possesses the weather-altering capability. Then again, DARPA denies that HAARP and the experiments going on up there have military applications at all—outside of communicating with subs and tidying up outer space after a high-altitude nuclear showdown.

WEIRD SCIENCE = WEIRD WEATHER?

Considering that it's the planet's most cutting-edge research project whatever its goals are, HAARP—an eerie 35-acre sci-fi forest of 180 antennae each shooting up 72 feet— sure doesn't get much attention. It blipped in the *Washington Post* and the *New York Times* in 1995 in articles about research communicating with submarines; years later it was mentioned in a brief sentence in a movie review of *Holes in Heaven*—a slick documentary narrated by Martin Sheen that questions HAARP's effects and potential uses as a weather-making machine and more. It pops up in *Wired* online most frequently—in articles that paint those questioning the project as "tin foil hatters" inter-spersed with occasional articles that wonder whether, hmmm, maybe they were right, at least about the military applications long denied. Knocking out satellites, jamming communications, and scouring underground with radio waves for hidden weapons and bunkers are a few uses mentioned in an unclassified DoD document "HAARP Research and Application" dug up by Above Top Secret.[48]

Officially the metal forest is a small "ionospheric heater" that shoots radio waves through a transmitter pointing hundreds of miles above, toasting bits of the ionosphere for minutes at a time—all in an effort to understand how these upper levels, where the ionosphere meets outer space, actually work and how they would affect communications during nuclear war. The HAARP facility can also shoot radio waves deep into the ground—capable of discerning underground weapons as well as deposits of oil and gas. It can also beam radio waves at satellites—rendering them useless—and could theoretically interfere with communications systems on aircraft. Some fret that radio waves could even be used to change moods. What exactly HAARP has done isn't well documented—but its powers are so vast that whenever there's an earthquake, some point to Alaska.

What is actually going on at HAARP isn't well scrutinized, says Begich, who is quick to distance himself from those who believe HAARP is responsible for every bout of weird weather. The facility, he says, does have disturbing capabilities—one being that it can cause instability within fault zones. If radio waves are beamed into the earth and "hit the right frequency, the right harmonic, they can trigger an earthquake," he says. "Was HAARP designed to do that? I don't know. Can it do that? Yes, it can. Can it be used to modify weather? Absolutely!"[49]

The facility "is not designed to be an operation system for military purposes," says the HAARP Internet site—and at least on that point the Air Force Research Lab, the Office of Naval

Research, and DARPA, which jointly oversee the project, and anti-HAARP activists led by Nick Begich agree. Begich and other anti-HAARP activists who have been making noise about it for fifteen years say that HAARP is merely a prototype, a glimpse of frightening things to come.

HAARP isn't the only unusual weapon that the Defense Department is funding that might alter the environment. Remote-controlled and genetically altered insects and mammals are among the experiments, and every so often they escape into the outside world. Drones are only the prototype for autonomous weapons, with an onboard computer that can communicate and fire on its own. Microwaves are being experimentally pulsed as crowd controllers and to knock out computers. Lasers aren't just for eye surgery—they're turning up in developmental airborne weapons. And atom smashers that can create mini-black holes don't sound eco-friendly, though the European Center for Nuclear Research, which oversees the facility in Switzerland, where the world's biggest smasher—the Large Hadron Collider—is currently smashing protons, assure us there's absolutely nothing to fret about.

2012 has become synonymous with the end of the world—and indeed human civilization is engaging in numerous activities that threaten the planet. We're throwing Earth's systems alarmingly out of whack as we're hitting the planetary limits—with oil and water being but two resources that are growing scarce. Even food is becoming an issue. Beyond the facts that one-fifth of the world's population doesn't get enough to eat and that one-third of Americans are obese, beyond wasteful irrigation practices and the overfishing that is killing off species, and beyond the concentration of farms in the hands of agribusiness, we're introducing genetically modified plants that not only travel to other fields and overtake them, but are leased by the year, giving control of the green food chain to companies such as Monsanto.

The world population is galloping and now nearing 7 billion—seven times greater than the population in 1800 and four times greater than that in 1900: the global count was a billion fewer a decade ago, at the turn of twenty-first century. And a fifth of the world's population live in poverty and without access to clean drinking water. Tropical forests are vanishing at the rate of one acre per second thanks to slash-and-burn farming as well as foraging for fuel, agribusiness, mining, and corporate activities; those forests, which cover 7 percent of the world's land, are crucial to the planet's nitrogen cycle and for absorbing carbon dioxide. Their rapid felling is now instead the source of 12 percent of global greenhouse gas emissions—a larger percentage than all ground vehicles put together. The planet's diverse plant and animal species—half of which dwell in the forests—are disappearing with the foliage. "A mass extinction is under way," the World Resources Institute reported in late 2009. Three species an hour go the way of the dinosaur—and by century's end, predicts the institute, half of our plants will be gone.[50]

And nuclear proliferation continues: nuclear arms never went out of fashion, and they are trendier than ever today. At least nine countries possess them, most everybody wants them—and the desire for them is often masked under the guise of a peaceful nuclear plant and fuel-making accessories, says disarmament expert Theresa Hitchens.[51]

A 2012 KIND OF MOOD

Psychologists say the deadly formula for suicide is a feeling of helplessness coupled with a feeling of hopelessness. That's what the doomsday portrayal of 2012 can instill, and it's all wrapped up with fear, which is absolutely the worst state of mind in which to make a decision. What's more, the 2012 phenomenon isn't enlightening: it's depressing, it's disempowering, and it's draining. And it's so thickly woven with fabrications and threads of half-truths that it's exhausting to try to unweave fact from fiction and psychotic babbling.

Myth makers peddling 2012—even idealists who paint 13.0.0.0.0 as a liftoff point—often twist reality, starting with repeated utterances about "prophecies" that don't exist. Their tales elicit a passive acceptance of our fate: We're smacked with 2012 scenarios that portray a world out of control, and certainly out of our control. Our world is going to be torched in fires, sucked into giant tsunamis, swept away in cruel floods, and enveloped by searing waves of molten lava. The solid earth below us will crumble and shake us into oblivion as the ground cracks beneath our feet; a comet is going to slam into us—on 12/21/12, when gravity and magnetism are also going to go goofy, the poles will violently and instantaneously reverse with north turning south—because the Earth is dangerously aligned with the sun and traversing a hazardous bit of the Milky Way. With cataclysm fated and foretold, there's little to do but flip out and maybe start humming with José, or perhaps arm thyself thoroughly and prepare to fight over resources, from farmland to water.

Granted, not all 2012-ers push an apocalyptic ending. Some say that due to energy streaming in from portals and planetary positioning, we will suddenly evolve, stop lying, and turn psychic. Such a graceful leap, beyond being hard to imagine, dismisses the need to actually confront the problems before us—problems that humming and hoping are not going to erase.

Indeed, humanity is in a pickle. But it's possible for us to lessen the throbbing of our self-inflicted global migraines—if we seriously acknowledge what we're doing and make a commitment to change.

The 2012 phenomenon has one beneficial outcome: It underscores the idea that human life on Earth is a luxury, not necessarily "a given" for millennia to come. Yet, 2012 peddlers essentially act as physicians who, after predicting that a patient will croak in ten years if he doesn't stop smoking, prescribe jellybeans and CDs of singing whales rather than recommend quitting.

Science, while responsible for our jams, also holds solutions—from stem cells for healing to algae for toxic cleanups. However, science alone isn't the answer. Drastic alteration of global behavior is required—from rearranging settlement patterns to planning for impacts of climate change. We also need to rethink our practice of siphoning off our most brilliant minds and trillions of dollars to develop arms and novel ways to destroy each other. In the same way that valuable human resources are wasted seeking out methods of ruination instead of directing people to the task of survival, the answers provided by 2012 leaders—think rainbows, stock up on canned goods, and/or pray—misdirect energies and drain the impetus to tackle our woes. And in so doing, they turn fears of devastation into potentially self-fulfilling prophecies.

05

CHANGE

TIME

At the end of the day, what can one conclude about the meaning of 2012 and the Long Count calendar that turns over that fateful year? Even if the mystics and trippy shamans appear to be drawing their warnings of doomsday and promises of insta-evolution from thin air, even if the Maya themselves never prophesied that the end date would come with celestial fireworks and planetary catastrophe, it is unnerving that the calendar is turning over in such a distressing and turbulent time, when even scientists are saying the planetary alarm clock is ringing in our ears demanding that we wake up if we are to survive.

And who knows—perhaps that isn't mere coincidence. Maybe the ancient mathematician-stargazers uncovered something that we've missed: Perhaps as we evolve in our understanding of the fourth dimension of time, quantum physics, and string theory (which postulates that there are at least ten interconnected dimensions of our world including time), we will discover that there is something significant about cycles of 5,125 years—the duration, more or less, of modern human civilization.

It's uncanny that the Long Count calendar appears to have started during an era of intense climate change, when humans were forced to change their ways and adapt, and appears to be ending exactly the same way.

The start date of the Long Count calendar in 3114 B.C. (a year that was apparently back-dated, as neither the Maya nor the calendar's creators, the Olmec, were around then) falls in a key era of human development. Scientists now say that right around that time, the planet underwent severe climactic change, including increased aridity. Anthropologists, social historians, and scientists now believe that the sudden water shortage tested humans, forcing them to change and adapt, as they migrated from small villages—with perhaps a dozen families living together on one or two acres—to river valleys with more reliable water sources. This migration prompted the first cities to spring up across the Middle East around 3000 B.C.E. The overarching priority of the settlements, where tens of thousands now spread over hundreds of acres, was to provide water: Complex irrigation and canal systems were the hallmarks of these new cities and city-states, which proved to be the building blocks of human civilization.

From that first step in collective resource management, "civilized" *Homo sapiens* were born. Cities sparked the human spirit—bringing out its best and worst. Walled urban centers soon provided both security and markets for new goods and triggered a spontaneous combustion of ideas. Language was written for the first time, novel technologies (including the potter's wheel) developed, materials such as bronze were developed, trade expanded as traders could travel long distances and leave behind families in relative safety, and improved farming techniques coaxed surpluses of food from the ground. The city quickly illustrated the benefits of collective humanity—sparking a burst of creativity, know-how, and shared resources and triggering jumps not only in wealth, but also in knowledge and the ability to understand and manipulate our external environment.

Cities also gave new intensity and scale to humanity's problems, woes that still plague us today: With tens of thousands of people living closely together, disease spread more easily; pollution—of water resources and even solid waste became an issue. What's more, cities brought power struggles as individuals and clans violently rose as wannabe leaders, and the urban centers literally encouraged war, making organized warfare possible for the first time: Not only was it easy to organize soldiers to pluck riches from less-protected villages, but cities themselves became sitting ducks, perpetuating the need for a war machine. As Lewis Mumford notes in *The City in History*, ". . . war [became] one of the reasons for the city's existence [and] the city's own wealth and power made it a natural target. The presence of thriving cities gave collective aggression a visible object that had never beckoned before: The city itself, with its growing accumulation of tools and mechanical equipment, its hoards of gold, silver and jewels . . . its well-filled granaries and storehouses . . ."[52] Ongoing conflict led to the development of an armed warrior class and turned creativity and resources to arms and security. This was the human world right around the time when the Long Count calendar began.

Flash to 5,125 years or so later. From the earliest Mesopotamian markets, we've developed a global marketplace, and the trader expeditions that once set out on foot now embark on 747s. Goods that once traveled on camels and small boats are now packed on trains and container ships. The early ability to manipulate our world by harnessing water has evolved into skill in manipulating the smallest particles of matter. We can travel—if not physically, then with our eyes—to destinations millions of light years away, recording the results in photos. Shamans and witches have been replaced by doctors and scientists as we are learning how to tap the body's ability to heal itself, though often the cure is found by cooking up compounds in the barks and roots that were used by the ancients.

Despite these advances, we are still grappling with the same issues that the first cities raised—on the upside, the tremendous potential unleashed by human cooperation, resource sharing, and skillful management, and on the downside, the hazards of scarcity and poor resource planning, the ravages of disease, greed, power plays, wars, and the sapping of creative forces and destruction of the environment in the race to devise new and better arms. The only difference appears to be the ability to recover: Five thousand years ago the world population was a few million, today it's 7 billion; back then a polluted or desiccated river could be abandoned for a fresh one, today we've tapped out the world's water resources. Today epidemics don't wipe out a city-state, they become global pandemics; and back then the might of all the arms in the world couldn't bring about planetary demise, while just a fraction of our arsenal could easily do so now.

As this cycle of the Long Count calendar draws to a close, perhaps the best way to approach 2012 is with a moment of deep, serious self-evaluation. We need to figure out how we can change to better adapt—and to lessen the likelihood of annihilation from war, resource depletion, and/or climate change. Because, however you look at it, humanity seems to be roaring to a crossroads, just as it was around 3000 B.C.E. It appears we are being asked to alter behavior—this time to live within the rules and means of the planet (which can only tolerate so much pollution and manipulation) and to address the activities that most jeopardize us—greed, lack of foresight, and war.

The leading cause for alarm isn't what's going to happen on December 21, 2012, it's our sluggishness to change in the years leading up to that date and beyond. That's why all the hoopla surrounding 2012 can appear to be a cop-out and self-fulfilling prophecy: Humming, visualization, and adopting a lunar calendar are probably not going to propel the sort of change that we need. Whether peddled by New Agers or zealots, academics or Hollywood movie makers, 2012 has become a fearful fix of an answer to the question of how we manage our world. Yes, one way or another the future could be rocky—that message has been hammered in—but the details are skimmed over by most 2012-ers, who ignore hands-on ideas for addressing problems: Oops, nothing left to do except passively await the grand finale, when we will all be destroyed or effortlessly make an evolutionary jump, becoming telepathic, unable to tell lies, and suddenly in harmony with both the Earth and extraterrestrials as we're energized by a photon beam.

Obsession with the end of the world isn't helping either. In fact it might be making it worse. Scientific studies show that our intentions can shape our reality: Thoughts and expectations shape outcomes. For example, experiments on light split through prisms show that the way observers expect the light to appear—as a wave or pillow-like "packet" of energy—dictates the way the light appears as it passes through.[53] The old truism holds. There is such a force as mind over matter, just not necessarily in the way the New Agers would have us believe.

In short, those who have decided that the world is ending—and refuse to participate in any solutions to forestall this outcome—may indeed hasten the end. The opposite holds true for those who care to heed the call to speed up attempts to prevent our demise.

2012—which has come to mean so many far-out things—may be laughed off as ridiculous, but the strangest thing about it is that regardless of the route to the conclusion, the year may well be a very odd one. As the clock ticks ever more loudly in the countdown to December 21, 2012—as José Argüelles, Daniel Pinchbeck, and John Major Jenkins organize tours to sacred Maya sites where they will hum and meditate expectantly on the heady day billed as the most transformational and hazardous ever—what should we remember, what should we expect? Will it be just another Y2K-like doomsday that comes and goes, or is 2012 somehow different? Whatever happens, it is clear that humanity hovers at a threshold that demands change.

In the end, maybe the message of the Maya is simply to adapt, not to repeat their mistake of ignoring the climate change that ultimately did them in, and for us to wake up—so they can go back to sleep.

Endnotes

[1] Self-proclaimed evangelical prophets Bob and Bonnie Jones are among the pushers of this idea. See Bob and Bonnie Jones, "Apostolic Government by 2012" (November 2008) on the Elijah List Web site: http://www.elijahlist.com/words/display_word/6873.

[2] See the translation of German magazine *Tattva Viveka* and the interview with José Argüelles conducted by editor Ronald Engert here: http://www.earthportals.com/Portal_Messenger/votan.html.

[3] Ibid.

[4] Ibid. Also see Michael Moynihan, "Visionary of the New Time: Michael Moynihan speaks with José Argüelles," *New Dawn*, November/December 2002, http://www.newdawnmagazine.com/articles/Interview%20With%20Jose%20Arguelles.html.

[5] John Major Jenkins, "What Is the Galactic Alignment?" undated article on his alignment 2012 site. See http://alignment2012.com/whatisga.htm.

[6] See Troy Anderson, "Doomsday at the Cineplex," *Christianity Today*, November 10, 2009, http://www.christianitytoday.com/ct/movies/news/2009/doomsday2012.html?start=1.

[7] See Jack Van Impe's DVD: *December 21st 2012: History's Final Day?*

[8] Anderson, "Doomsday at the Cineplex."

[9] Ibid.

[10] See Bob Frissell, *Something in this Book Is True* (Berkeley, CA: Frog Ltd., 1997).

[11] John Major Jenkins, *Maya Cosmogenesis 2012: The True Meaning of the Maya Calendar End-Date* (Rochester, VT: Bear & Company, 1998).

[12] "Severe Space Weather Events—Understanding Societal and Economic Impacts," Workshop Report, Space Studies Board, National Research Council, National Academy of Sciences. (Washington, D.C.: National Academies Press, 2008).

[13] Robert L. Christiansen et al., *Preliminary Assessment of Volcanic and Hydrothermal Hazards in Yellowstone National Park and Vicinity.* (Washington, D.C.: USGS, Department of the Interior, 2007).

[14] "Sea Levels Rising Faster Than Earlier Forecasts, Scientists Say," *Bloomberg*, November 24, 2009, http://www.bloomberg.com/apps/news?pid=20601081&sid=aU6tyGmdGPPQ.

[15] "Friday the 13th, 2029," NASA, May 13, 2004, http://science.nasa.gov/science-news/science-at-nasa/2005/13may_2004mn4/.

[16] "Satellites Reveal a Mystery of Large Change in Earth's Gravity Field," NASA, August 1, 2001, http://gsfc.nasa.gov/topstory/2002/20020801gravityfield.html.

[17] Linda Schele and David Freidel, *A Forest of Kings: The Untold Story of the Ancient Maya* (New York: Harper Perennial, 1990).

[18] Jenkins, *Maya Cosmogenesis 2012*, p. xli.

[19] For more background, see "Breaking the Maya Code: Interview with Michael Coe" transcript, Nightfire Films, 2005, http://www.nightfirefilms.org/breakingthemayacode/interviews/CoeTRANSCRIPT.pdf.

[20] Excerpt from John Lloyd Stephens, *Incidents of Travel in Central America, Chiapas, and Yucatán*, first published in 1841.

[21] The CIA admits to its involvement in the coup. The introduction to CIA documents found on the agency's Freedom of Information Act Pages begins, "This collection—5,120 documents (over 14,000 pages)—chronicles CIA involvement in the 1954 coup in Guatemala. These records encompass the events and circumstances causing U.S. policymakers to plan the overthrow of the Guatemalan Government in June 1954 as Cold War tensions mounted between the two superpowers, the U.S. and Soviet Union; CIA plans for and execution of the covert action; the outcome; and CIA historical analysis of CIA's performance and impact of the coup. The collection includes reviews of the event by CIA historians, administrative memos regarding operational plans and internal approvals; operational cable traffic; and summaries of the Sherwood tapes used for propaganda purposes." See http://www.foia.cia.gov/guatemala.asp.

[22] Interview with author, August 2009.

[23] Sergio Ortiz, "Rescuing Regal Ruins," *Americas*, September–October 2004.

[24] Tami Simon (editor). *The Mystery of 2012.* (Boulder, CO: Sounds True, 2007). As translated by Robert K. Sitler, noted Maya scholar, in his essay "2012 and the Maya World," p. 97.

[25] Ibid.

[26] Walter Sullivan, "New Era Dawns—Or Just a New Day," *New York Times,* August 11, 1987.

[27] Jim Ritter. "Big Days Here for 'New Age' Cult," *Chicago Sun-Times*, August 9, 1987.

[28] Moynihan, "Interview with José Argüelles," *New Dawn.*

[29] See http://www.lawoftime.org/lawoftime.html.

[30] "The 2012 Peace Plan," from the Galactic Research Institute site: http://www.lawoftime.org/2012/2012.html.

[31] Moynihan, "Interview with José Argüelles," *New Dawn.*

[32] An article in a January 1999 issue of *Christianity Today* notes that a number of evangelical preachers were stirring up fear about the approach of the twenty-first century, among them Jerry Falwell, who "predicted God's wrath on January 1, 2000." The article quotes Falwell as delivering a sermon in August 1998 in which he said the Lord "may be preparing to confound our language, to jam our communications, scatter our efforts, and judge us for our sin and rebellion against his lordship. We are hearing from many sources that January 1, 2000, will be a fateful day in the history of the world." See Mark A. Kellner, "The Coming Secular Apocalypse," *Christianity Today*, January 11, 1999: http://www.christianitytoday.com/ct/1999/january11/9t1054.html?start=2.

[33] Carl Johan Calleman, PhD, "The Nine Underworlds: Expanding Levels of Consciousness," *The Mystery of 2012*, (Boulder, CO: Sounds True, 2007).

[34] Preface to Jenkins, *Maya Cosmogenesis.*

[35] Ibid.

[36] From Argüelles's Web site: www.lawoftime.org. See "Timeship Earth 2013."

[37] "Even the Maya Are Getting Sick of 2012 Hype," MSNBC, October 10, 2009, http://www.msnbc.msn.com/id/33261483/.

[38] Victoria Jaggard, "Magnetic-Shield Cracks Found; Big Solar Storms Expected," *National Geographic News*, December 17, 2008, http://news.national geographic.com/news/2008/12/081217-solar-breaches.html. Also note that the problem of incoming solar plasma is exacerbated by a recent solar magnetic reversal; acting with the Earth's magnetic shield, the solar magnetics essentially help to further open up the magnetosphere.

[39] Interview with author, September 2009.

[40] "Operation Argus: Fact Sheet" from Defense Threat Reduction Agency; http://www.dtra.mil/documents/ntpr/factsheets/Argus.pdf; also see "Operation Argus, 1958 Report," http://www.dtra.mil/rd/programs/nuclear_personnel/ docs/DNA6039F.pdf.

[41] Rosalie Bertell, "Background on the HAARP Project," Global Policy Forum, November 5, 1996, http://www.globalpolicy.org/component/content/article/ 212/45492.html.

[42] Ibid.

[43] Ibid. Also supported by "Operation Argus: Fact Sheet."

[44] Interview with author, September 2009.

[45] Ignatius Donnelly, *Ragnarok: Age of Fire and Gravel*, originally published 1883, Project Gutenberg, 2002: http://www.gutenberg.org/etext/5109.

[46] "Cohen Address at Conference on Terrorism, Weapons of Mass Destruction, and U.S. Strategy," Sam Nunn Policy Forum, April 28, 1997, University of Georgia, Athens, Georgia: http://www.fas.org/news/usa/1997/04/bmd970429d.htm.

[47] Interview with author, September 2009.

[48] See http://foia.abovetopsecret.com/ultimate_UFO/Advanced/HAARP ResearchAndApplications.com.

[49] Interview with author, September 2009.

[50] Richard Kahle, "The 6th Extinction and Protected Areas," *EarthTrends*, October 2, 2009: http://earthtrends.wri.org/updates/node/356.

[51] Interview with author, September 2009.

[52] Lewis Mumford, *The City in History* (New York: Penguin, 1991).

[53] Gregg Braden, "Choice Point 2012," *The Mystery of 2012* (Boulder, CO: Sounds True, 2007).

Index